FOREIGN EXCHANGE: THE COMPLETE DEAL

A COMPREHENSIVE GUIDE TO THE THEORY AND PRACTICE OF THE FOREX MARKET

By James Sharpe

HARRIMAN HOUSE LTD
3A Penns Road
Petersfield
Hampshire
GU32 2EW
GREAT BRITAIN

Tel: +44 (0)1730 233870
Fax: +44 (0)1730 233880
Email: enquiries@harriman-house.com
Website: www.harriman-house.com

First published in Great Britain in 2012

ISBN: 978–1906–659–65–3

British Library Cataloguing in Publication Data
A CIP catalogue record for this book can be obtained from the British Library.

Printed and bound in the UK by CPI Group (UK) Ltd, Croydon, CR0 4YY

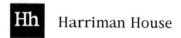 Harriman House

Thanks to G. Ashley, P. Balans, C. Crispin, J. Elston

CONTENTS

To Victoria, Katharine, James and Olivia

PREFACE

People have been exchanging money for generations but it is only in the last 100 years or so that currency trading as we would recognise has taken place. It could even be reasonably argued that it is only really in the last 40 years, with the removal of exchange controls, the emergence of floating exchange rates, and improvements in communications, that the market as we know it today fully evolved.

Concurrent with this, and equally important, has been the development of multinational companies and the inexorable rise in government traded debt. The explosive growth of cross-border investment, both direct and portfolio, has brought with it foreign exchange exposures to be managed, often proactively. It is the rapid changes in communications and computing power, though, which have forged the features of the 21st cenutry market, and created a mjaor role for the speculator (both professional and private) – we now have 24-hour dealing and *daily* foreign exchange turnover in excess of $4trn.

This book is firmly rooted in foreign exchange but I am very much of the mind that markets should be viewed in a holistic fashion – to treat foreign exchange as somehow isolated from the other markets would be a crucial error. It is important to grasp the relationship between the foreign exchange market, in whatever guise, bond and equity performance, national interests and ultimately economic management.

The importance of these relationships is an underlying theme of the book and in this context the initial chapters will explore the historical and theoretical background to the foreign exchange market. My starting point is the end of the First World War in 1918. Since that time, the management of exchange rates and their volatility has become integral to economic performance and indeed to the political landscape.

In less than 100 years, perceptions have altered such that market movements that would previously have been viewed as inevitable or plain economic misfortune are now deemed to be mismanagement. It may then come as no surprise that even in a largely floating rate system central banks continue to directly influence foreign exchange markets. I also provide an invaluable insight to what determines exchange rates. These opening chapters provide a platform for an understanding of the practice of foreign exchange, which is the core of the book. I recommend you read and digest these opening chapters, but if you do wish to skip the history and move straight to the practice of foreign exchange you can do so by starting with chapter 3.

In subsequent chapters, the practical aspects of foreign exchange will be examined in a manner that will leave readers with a clear understanding of the issues and processes involved in foreign exchange transactions. Spot, forwards, non-deliverable forwards, bid-offer spreads and pips, among other concepts, will be explained with straightforward examples and simple arithmetic.

I shall show the methods used to execute transactions, including orders, and how a bank actually deals on the other side. I shall look at whether we should deal directly with the bank or use trading platforms which have proliferated in recent years, and I will discuss how best to choose and manage the relationship with foreign exchange providers. I shall also show how professional traders analyse markets and provide a blueprint for professional trading.

In chapter 7 I look at the subject of price prediction, or *forecasting*. Market forecasters unfortunately have a distinct tendency to err but still prosper on people's insatiable demand to know the future. As there is no firm basis of knowledge to hold prices steady, they are subject to sudden and violent changes, which makes prediction difficult. There have been improvements in computing power and coverage of the markets is at an all-time high, but this does not necessarily make them any easier to interpret. I will also look at the growth in technical analysis trading models, which has been assisted by vastly enhanced computer power in recent years.

Foreign exchange can appear remarkably simple, after all there are just two numbers to choose from, and you can either buy, sell or do nothing, but it is important to recognise that foreign exchange is not solely a numbers game. Foreign exchange numbers are driven by a large number of complicated factors, including human psychology, and understanding them requires not so much a grasp of the economic fundamentals as of the irrational way in which people can behave when they join together in crowds. After reading this book you will be in a better position to plan and react to the foreign exchange markets.

This book is intended for the business school student, banker or private investor as well as for corporate treasurers and fund managers. It is my intention that it should be invaluable in unravelling the jargon and mystique of foreign exchange.

1.

EXCHANGE RATE SYSTEMS: FROM FIXED TO FLOATING, AND CHAOS

An exchange rate system is any system which determines the conditions under which one currency can be exchanged for another. Fixed, floating and adjustable peg systems (of which there are various) are the three main systems available. All systems are designed to facilitate trade and investment across national boundaries.

To understand the foreign exchange systems in the 21st century we need to see where we have come from and why. In this overview I will start from the end of the First World War, which allows us to look at all the main examples of exchange rate systems up to the present day. In essence, every generation has wrestled with the same problem: namely, how to set up an effective system to determine how exchange rates should be calculated and how deficits should be financed.

No system has been without its problems, hence the variety of approaches that have been developed, although these problems have as much to do with an extraordinary passage of events in this period as to specific defects in any particular system. These events include two World Wars, the Korean War, the Vietnam War, the Cold War, the Great Depression, oil shocks and rampant inflation. Over this period the social and political landscape has changed dramatically; political accountability is now widespread and, as mentioned in the preface, events that would have been viewed as inevitable or just economic misfortune in the past are now judged to be mismanagement. For this reason I have paid particular attention to the role of central banks, especially their intervention in the markets.

While the period is littered with crises I have only covered pivotal moments, or events that illustrate a key issue. It is not intended to be a complete history of foreign exchange but rather to provide a rich insight into what actually drives the foreign exchange markets. Each generation is inclined to view its circumstances as something unprecedented or unique, but, as we will see, this is rarely the case.

At the end of the chapter, the overview of the route from fixed exchange rates to a floating rate system is followed by a specific look at the UK foreign exchange experience since 1960.

This chapter will make some reference to countries' *current accounts* and, therefore, before we move on to the historical overview of the transition from fixed exchange rates to floating exchange rates, it is important to introduce the idea of current accounts here.

National current accounts

The current account of a country is made up of the difference between the worth of exports and imports (visibles) and the difference in trade in services, e.g., insurance, shipping, banking and investment income (invisibles). Current account deficits (where imports are worth more than exports) are generally seen as a sign of economic weakness, with surpluses (where exports are worth more than imports) viewed as the opposite. This is rather simplistic but it provides a useful starting point.

A current account deficit may occur because of government spending, or spending by private firms and individuals. A deficit, whoever is generating it, will need to be financed. This is either through increased borrowing overseas or by a reduction in investments overseas. Debt in itself is not bad. Borrowings may increase the productive potential of the economy, particularly in a development context. Also, debt may be rising but actually falling as a percentage of Gross National Product (GNP). This normally will not create problems.

However, if the deficit is rising as a percentage of the economy there comes a point when lenders start to worry about the risk of default and refuse to lend more. During this process the cost of borrowing will inevitably rise. Examples of this were provided by Greece, Portugal and Ireland in 2010 and 2011. This can prompt an enforced adjustment where further funding, for example from the International Monetary Fund (IMF) or European Union (EU), is conditional upon cuts in spending, including pension and welfare provisions. Apart from the economic implications – such as a short-term negative impact on employment and growth – this has a political downside as it can lead to demonstrations and civil unrest.

The US experience is a special case in so far as the US dollar is the world's reserve currency, meaning that it is the currency most other countries use to pay their debts. Spiralling deficits, however, have raised doubts about whether this can continue. More debt will tend to lead to higher costs for the issuer and overseas investors may lose their appetite for funding the deficit by buying dollars, at least at the current exchange rate. As C. Fred Bergsten rather succinctly put it:

> It has long been known that large external deficits pose substantial risks to the US economy because foreign investors might at some point refuse to finance these deficits on terms compatible with US prosperity. Any sudden stop in lending to the United States would drive the dollar down, push inflation and interest rates up, and perhaps bring on a hard landing for the United States – and the world economy at large.[1]

This was very much the concern of the US Treasury and Federal Reserve in 2008 when a collapsing dollar was putting at risk the US bond and asset markets.

When the point at which overseas investors refuse to lend any more is reached, countries are forced to return the current account to balance, usually through cutting down on imports, expanding exports, depressing domestic consumption and depressing living standards. This adjustment process is usually relatively short. However, the readjustment forces on sub-Saharan economies in the early 1980s were to have a negative impact for decades.

Some countries (such as Japan and China) run large sustained current account surpluses via the trade balance. This has benefits of increased investment income. A number of oil-producing countries have created funds for future generations from the surpluses, e.g., Norway, Kuwait and Abu Dhabi. The problem with large prolonged surpluses is that they inevitably lead to friction between countries over jobs and exports. Surpluses invested in government bonds are not especially politically sensitive as they have little visibility to the electorate but this soon changes when iconic buildings and flagship companies are bought.

In the 2000s, China has regularly faced accusations of an undervalued currency, manipulated by the authorities, being used to generate enormous surpluses. This has been hotly disputed by the Chinese authorities who, nevertheless, most notably from 2003, have regularly sold the Chinese Renminbi and bought dollars. These imbalances are effectively a savings gap. The US consumes too much, and saves too little; China is saving too much and forgoing consumption. In this context Chinese savings are being used to plug the US deficit through US Treasury purchases.

---

[1] C. Fred Bergsten, Director of the P G Peterson Institute for International Economics.

These imbalances create volatility in the foreign exchange markets in times of crisis as investors repatriate funds (such as in 2008) and if it is felt the currency valuation is seriously at odds with fair value. Global imbalances require global solutions but to date political consensus has not been achieved. Policies that have a negative impact on domestic employment, even in the short term, are not easily embraced. In practice the situation early in the 21st century is not that different to the 1930s, when countries looked to devalue their currencies in order to gain competitive advantage.

A natural partner to protectionism is a global economic and financial crisis leading to a sharp drop in global trade volumes. The 1930s is an obvious example but trade tensions were very evident in 2002 (following the 2001 recession) and in 2009. An indicator in the last two cases is the number of complaints to the World Trade Organisation (WTO), which rose sharply. For example, Europe was increasingly vocal on China. European Central Bank (ECB) President Trichet said in March 2010: "the message is that progressive and orderly appreciation of the Chinese currency would be both in the interest of China and the interest of the global economy".

There are no recent examples of a full trade war but the impact can be surmised. Protectionist policies will reduce the potential growth of an economy and in a global economic recession protectionism can lengthen the downturn and hinder any recovery. The leading industrialised nations (the members of the G7 and G20) have increasingly looked to the IMF to provide currency surveillance to prevent such circumstances, but not a great deal has come of this as yet.

With the concept of the current account and its importance introduced, I now move on to the overview of exchange rate systems since 1918. This begins with a look at fixed exchange rates.

FIXED EXCHANGE RATES

A fixed exchange rate system is one where a currency has a fixed value against another currency or commodity. The implied purpose of fixed exchange rate systems is to unite the global economic performance and policies of nations. The best known example of a fixed system was the gold standard which operated in the 19th and early 20th centuries.

The gold standard

In 1914 a holder of a £1 note could go to the Bank of England and exchange the note for 0.257 ounces of gold. Similar practices existed in other European countries and the USA, which meant that there was a fixed exchange rate between the major trading currencies.

The key element in the adjustment mechanism was that domestic money supply in a country was directly related to the amount of gold held by the country's central bank. If the UK was running a deficit there was a net outflow of pounds from the country. When these pounds in turn were exchanged for gold at the Bank of England there would be a net outflow of gold from the UK. With the reduction in gold, the Bank of England would have to make a corresponding reduction of notes in circulation. This led to a reduction in money supply as cash was withdrawn, a rise in interest rates, a reduction in loans, a weakening of prices, and cutbacks in output and employment. Meanwhile, the gold arriving in Paris or Berlin (for example) would prompt an opposite pattern: the expansion of loans activity and an associated rise in prices.

In this example, the fall in demand in the UK would reduce imports, and exports would become more competitive as prices fell. Employment would be restored, the current account would be returned to equilibrium and another cycle would begin. A deficit on the current account could not be corrected by a devaluation of the currency (as it might be in 2011) because under the gold standard mechanism the currency was fixed in value. Imbalances were corrected through deflation and reflation via interest rates and fiscal policy.

In effect the First World War marked the beginning of the end of the standard as the belligerent powers were forced to reduce their gold holdings to pay for US weaponry and wheat. US gold stocks at the end of 1914 stood at $1.5bn but by the end of 1917 they were valued at $2.9bn. In practice there was no longer a workable distribution of gold stocks because there was abundance in the US and paucity almost everywhere else.

Efforts to revive the gold standard were made in the 1920s but with little success. After the First World War no major country allowed the free export of gold. This meant that domestic policy was no longer constrained by the fear that gold would go offshore. The prospect of reduced note circulation, bank loans, and the depressing impact on prices, employment and production had been removed. As such, countries were now free to pursue their own policies with no immediate regard for what other countries were doing. The coordinating discipline imposed by the gold standard (reinforced by a balanced budget mantra) had gone.

This is similar to the dilemmas facing international exchange management in the early part of the 21st century as the demise of the gold standard coincided with growing nationalism and a growing tendency to hold governments accountable for economic performance. Under this new freedom the greatest inflations of modern history in Germany and Austria occurred, as well as the rise of fascism and communism, protectionism, and the Great Depression.

The arguments in favour of a fixed rate revolve around certainty and economic discipline. Extreme volatility under a floating exchange rate system is regularly cited as its principal weakness. This is simply because in international business there is usually an element of futurity: deals are struck now against future payment. When a currency changes in price from day to day this introduces instability or uncertainty into trade, which affects prices and in turn sales. In a similar way, importers are unsure how much it is going to cost them to import a given amount of foreign goods. Related arguments are also applied to foreign investment flows, which involve the purchase or sale of equities, bonds, commercial interests and fixed assets, e.g., land and property.

This uncertainty can be reduced by hedging foreign exchange risk, and banks have created a panoply of products to resolve this problem, many of which are discussed later. These products have certainly reduced the negative impact of volatility on trade and investment. As we have seen, trade flows and current account balances have historically been the drivers of foreign exchange markets. Of growing importance is *real money* portfolio flows (bonds and equities) and any hedging that may be applied to these investments. Fund managers may hedge all, part or none of their exposure.

Bretton Woods and adjustable pegs

Before long – in fact prior to the end of the Second World War – it was recognised that a new international monetary framework was required in order to determine how exchange rates would be valued and how deficits would be financed. With the aim of resolving this dilemma, at Bretton Woods in 1944 the International Monetary Fund (IMF) was established and the member countries of the fund assented to have their currencies expressed either in terms of a given amount of gold or an amount of US dollars. Each member country agreed to see that these values were maintained within a given range. At the same time the US agreed with the IMF that its currency would always be convertible into gold and that it in turn would always buy and sell gold at a fixed price of $35 per ounce. This became the basis of the US dollar reserve function. The dollar had become the predominant medium for the settlement of international transactions.

For instance, from 1949 to 1967 the pound was valued at $2.80. This was known as par value for the currency. The Bank of England agreed to maintain prices within a 1% range so the pound could fluctuate from $2.78 to $2.82. If the price drifted below or above these levels the Bank of England would intervene in the market, buying or selling pounds as appropriate.

The Bretton Woods System is the best example of an adjustable peg system. In the short term, currencies are fixed in value against one another. In the longer term, currencies could be devalued or revalued if dictated by economic fundamentals. Exchange rate stability was maintained by buying and selling currencies and was therefore crucially dependent on gold and currency reserves held by the central banks.

Up to the late 1950s the US gold reserves exceeded the total dollar reserves of all foreign central banks by a ratio of 3:1. At this time the most typical response to heavy selling pressure on a currency was to raise interest rates. This attracted speculative flows from overseas, raising the demand for, and hence the price of, the currency. This could also be allied to exchange controls. The last resort, when reserves were depleted, was to borrow from the IMF. In practice governments tended to deflate their economies, reducing imports and hence restoring a current account balance.

The 1950s can viewed as a period of relative calm. With exchange rates set by Bretton Woods and tight exchange control regulations, trading opportunities were limited and dealers did little more than execute customer orders. Therefore, the dealing function of a bank attracted little interest. In the 1950s and through the late 1960s the US was the cornerstone around which international economic policy was based. The dollar played a role as a safe haven currency within a stable price environment. If a country faced an outflow of dollars it signalled the need to take corrective measures. This could be via tighter monetary and fiscal policies, incomes policies or even devaluation. At this time it was adjustment to the US that coordinated policies amongst the industrialised nations, which in turn provided the basis of international currency stability. The key point is that if stable exchange rates were desired, price levels had to be relatively stable, or at least moving in line with one another.

The pre-eminent position of the US, crafted from the two World Wars, was becoming strained in the 1960s as cost differences and levels of productivity started to widen between industrial countries. This was most visible in Germany and Japan. Post-war both countries channelled their savings into rebuilding new, efficient industrial plants, and arms expenditures were restricted by the victorious powers. This was coupled with significantly lower labour costs.

The US, in contrast, was channelling savings into military expenditures, which later increased further as a product of the Vietnam War. The result was that the dollar was fixed at an overvalued level and sales of goods from Germany and Japan flourished. The first cracks started to appear in the US economy by late 1958. From 1958 to 1960 the US ran up deficits of $11.2bn. This led to an accumulation of dollars held by foreign corporations, which in turn spawned the Euro-dollar market. A portion of these dollars were converted into gold and so began the reversal of the reserves the US had built up as a result of the First World War.

The emergence of the floating exchange rate system

In March 1968 the US established a two-tier market rate for gold in an effort to mitigate the drain on their gold reserves. In this system all central-bank transactions in gold were insulated from the free market price. Central banks would trade gold among themselves at $35 per troy ounce but would not trade with the private market. The private market could trade at the market price and there would be no official intervention. By 1970, however, US gold reserves were down to $11bn, a fall of around 61% in ten years.

The end came in August 1971, when there were massive outflows of dollars. Much of the speculative activity was in favour of the Deutschmark, partly due to relatively favourable interest rates. On 15 August 1971 President Nixon announced the closure of the gold window; in other words, the dollar would no longer be converted into gold. This effectively meant that the Bretton Woods Agreement to establish a new monetary order had foundered. Official parities and intervention points were suspended and most major currencies began a clean or managed float.

In December 1971 negotiations got underway at the Smithsonian Institution in Washington to arrange the devaluation and stabilisation of the dollar. Eventually new parities were agreed against the dollar. These reflected varying rates of devaluation for the dollar: approximately 17% for the yen, 13.6% for the Deutschmark, and, remarkably, 8.6% for sterling. The governments agreed to hold the exchange rates within a range of 2.25% of the agreed parities.

In early 1973 there was a further exodus out of dollars and in February 1973 the dollar was devalued by 10% and the official price of gold raised to $42.22 per ounce. Pressure still continued on the dollar, as inflation was on the rise as well as the prospect of further devaluation. In late 1973 the Yom Kippur War and the sudden increase in the price of oil caused further turmoil in the markets. The subsequent spike in inflation and the recession of 1974/75 created such payment imbalances that a return to fixed parities was impossible.

This ushered in a system of floating exchange rates.

FLOATING EXCHANGE RATES

In the 1970s currency instability emerged as the accepted policy and this received the benign nomenclature of a float. The 1974 Economic Report of the US President, summarising the move away from fixed exchange rates, read:

> The year 1973 may be characterised as one of continuing adjustment to past disequilibria. Early in the year the governments of most major countries abandoned attempts to fix exchange rates at negotiated levels. While central banks continued to intervene to some extent, foreign exchange markets played the major role in determining the exchange rates that would clear the market. The process was marked at times by unusually large fluctuations of market exchange rates.[2]

Note the reference to the key element in any definition of a free or floating exchange rate system – exchange rates are determined by free market forces. When a government intervenes in the foreign exchange market to influence exchange rates by buying or selling currency the system can be called a *managed float* or a *dirty float*. The float is *dirty* because there has been a deliberate interference with pure market forces of demand and supply.

Stability under the floating rate system

The fundamental flaw of the floating rate system, experienced on many occasions, is that exchange rates can move to levels far removed from any notion of long-term competitive levels. It could be argued that it is not correct to talk of undervaluation or overvaluation in a floating rate system. After all, it is the market that determines the level and it cannot be wrong. However, speculation is an inherent part of a floating system and this does create overvaluations and undervaluations in the exchange rate.

Overvaluations generate slumps in the internationally exposed sectors and can lead to deindustrialisation and protectionism, while undervaluations will generate inflationary pressures by allowing import prices to rise as the exchange rate falls. This has undoubtedly been the case for the UK, for example, which is dependent on imports of food and raw materials. It has also become an issue for a number of countries which are pegged to the dollar, notably those in the Middle East.

---

[2] **fraser.stlouisfed.org/publications/ERP/issue/1227**

Moreover, a rise in interest rates as part of an anti-inflation package may encourage an inflow of funds. This will increase the price of the currency and will make the economy less internationally competitive. These circumstances detract from satisfactory economic performance. In this context the exchange rate should guide the central bankers on when to ease up and when to restrain. The official mantra, however, is that stability rather than an appropriate level of the exchange rate is their objective. The G7 revealed this intention when it said on 3 October 2009:

> We confirm our shared interest in a strong and stable international financial system. Excess volatility and disorderly movements in exchange rates have adverse implications for economic and financial stability. We continue to monitor exchange rates closely, and cooperate as appropriate.

Governments have introduced the goal of economic convergence – sustainable non-inflationary economic growth – as the means to achieve this foreign exchange stability.

The choice of exchange rate system is extremely important as it determines the process and impact of any adjustment and indeed has become the focus of discussion within Europe. I shall now *look at these adjustment mechanisms in more detail.*

Adjustment mechanisms with floating exchange rates

The proponents of a floating exchange rate will cite its flexibility and self-correcting nature. With a floating exchange rate, a balance of payments disequilibrium should be rectified by a change in the external price of the currency – a self-correcting mechanism.

For example, if a country has a current account payments deficit then the currency should depreciate. The effect of the depreciation should be to make the country's exports cheaper and imports more expensive, thus increasing demand for goods abroad and reducing internal demand for foreign goods, therefore dealing with the balance of payments problem. Conversely, a balance of payments surplus should be eliminated by an appreciation of the currency.

However, recent experience in the UK and US indicates that a floating exchange rate does not automatically cure a balance of payments deficit, or at best the correction process is glacial. This is because the competitiveness of a country's economy is not just about the currency. Ultimately, the trade adjustment will have to go hand in hand with an adjustment in savings and consumption in each economy.

The adjustment mechanisms associated with fixed exchange rates versus floating exchange rates tend to produce different economic costs. Under a fixed rate system, curing a deficit is likely to involve a general deflationary policy (higher taxes, cuts in expenditures) resulting in increased unemployment and lower economic growth. The floating rate system tends to be inflationary as the exchange rate depreciates following current account deficits. This has usually been the case for countries such as the UK, which is dependent on imports of food and raw materials. It has become an issue for a number of countries which are pegged to the dollar, notably in the Middle East.

A rise in interest rates as part of an anti-inflation package may encourage an inflow of funds. This will increase the price of the currency and will make the economy less internationally competitive. Floating can therefore raise concerns over discipline in economic management. The presence of an inflation target though should help overcome this. When using a fixed rate system, governments have a built-in incentive not to follow inflationary policies. If they do, then unemployment and balance of payments problems are certain to result as the economy becomes uncompetitive.

For this reason, under the Bretton Woods Agreement governments could not allow their inflation rates to differ greatly. The initial policy response was normally to deflate; under the gold standard, deflation would have occurred automatically. Unemployment would rise in both cases. As Galbraith put it, those who express a preference between inflation and depression are "making a fool's choice – you deal with what you have". Deflation and depression in the 1930s and inflation in the 1970s were both destructive to the world order.

Those who prefer the floating system will claim that under fixed exchange rates there is loss of freedom in internal policy. This is clearly the case for those who joined the euro in January 1999. Some commentators in the UK regularly quote this as a good reason not to enter and cite the positive effects of devaluation post-1992 and the ability to devalue after the financial shocks of 2008. However, it begs the question of whether if there had been financial discipline prior to these events then devaluation would not have been an issue. In both cases the inflationary impact was muted as fortunately global deflationary pressures dominated.

Looking at the euro in more detail provides some interesting insights.

The euro experience

The euro experience has been broadly positive and the euro now ranks as the second reserve currency behind the dollar. The major criticism of it has been the one size-fits-all monetary policy, but this has also crucially been allied to failures to adjust fiscal policy. This was clearly evident in 2010 in Ireland, Greece and Portugal, which prompted a sell off in the euro and speculation of a break up of the entire union.

The need for fiscal convergence was recognised at the outset of the European Monetary Union but subsequently ignored or manipulated by politicians. The Maastricht Treaty signed in 1992 said that governments had to have budget deficits of no more than 3% of Gross Domestic Product (GDP) and a national debt of less than 60% of GDP (it was known as a stability pact). The importance of balance between monetary and fiscal policy has never been more clearly evident. Unfortunately, the euro-zone countries have behaved as if they were each managing their own currencies.

Each country appears to go its own way in raising taxes or borrowing money. In the past, imbalances would be adjusted over time through an appreciation or devaluation of the currency. This option is no longer available and in the case of Greece the only option was severe austerity measures, including cuts in wages and pensions.

Since the introduction of the Maastricht Treaty the deficit rules have been violated over 40 times. Greece tops the list in this respect. It has only once managed to push its deficit below 3% and this was through creative accounting in 2006. Also, Greece has raised debt through complex structures which have not been included in official statistics.

Ironically, it was Germany that was the second member state, after Portugal, to be subjected to an excessive deficit procedure by the European Union. It was also the German government who steered an "improvement in the implementation of the Stability and Growth Pact" at a special meeting of the Ecofin Council on 20 March 2005. This improvement could only be seen from a political viewpoint as it allowed more frequent exceptional and temporary violations of the deficit rules.

The Bundesbank declared that the changes would "decisively weaken the rules of sound financial policy" and the "goal of achieving sustainable public finances in all member states of the monetary union is being jeopardised". This judgement has been borne out by recent events in Greece and other periphery countries, notably Ireland and Portugal. It has highlighted that while there is a common monetary policy the members of the euro lack a coherent and credible shared economic policy. It has shown that even small countries can jeopardise the entire currency project. Politically, it has prompted a change in awareness that its members are dependent on one other.

CONCLUSION

Fixed exchange rates are not just about numbers. They signal intent for co-ordinating economic behaviour and financial discipline. At best they unite the economic performance and policies of nations. In the case of Europe and the USA they represent political integration. Floating is more a statement of self interest which of late has become polarised between the West and Asia. When the industrialised nations went over to floating in 1973 it was not because flexible exchange rates were regarded as a better system but simply because the system of fixed rates had temporarily collapsed.

Floating certainly has its advocates who would argue that it has coped well with oil crises and recession, and provided a more benign adjustment mechanism. This is important when set against the backdrop of the electorate holding governments increasingly accountable for economic performance. It has, however, seen the demise of financial discipline and has led to overshooting and undershooting of exchange prices, which is its major flaw. This has prompted active government intervention, although the primary stated ambition has been to stabilise disorderly markets rather than to create artificial exchange rates. The effectiveness of this intervention has not been firmly established.

During the period in question foreign exchange dealing has seen enormous changes. The rapid changes in communications and computing power has forged the 24-hour dealing market and the speculator; this pair is often blamed for chaotic markets. In reality 24-hour dealing and speculators are the symptom of the problem not the problem itself.

Increasingly wild fluctuations in the exchange rates, which is the situation in the 21st century, have little attraction in the medium term, both in terms of trade and asset allocation. The recent lessons from Europe, discussed in this chapter, are that to achieve stability the politicians will have to learn to live with financial discipline and take responsibility for managing electoral expectations.

FOREIGN EXCHANGE AND THE UK – 1960 TO THE 2000S

1960s

By the 1960s the deterioration in the UK's competitive position was becoming increasingly evident. This was partly a legacy of the war and partly due to an economy heavily dependent on trade, but it was also caused by an inability to change working practices and restructure industry to the new world order.

In 1964 the Labour Prime Minister Harold Wilson made the famous declaration that he would defend the sterling parity as established at Bretton Woods at $2.80. The inevitable revaluation away from $2.80 was stalled by various support packages but by 1967 (18 November) it was finally recognised that sterling was fundamentally overvalued and that the economy could not support the rate and so a devaluation of 14.3% was arranged. This reduced the parity rate from $2.80 to $2.40.

1970s

The sterling demise had been coming for some time; rising deficits, rampant inflation, political gridlock and industrial unrest on a grand scale (for example, the miners' strike) had become features of the 1970s. In December 1973 Idi Amin, the Ugandan dictator, launched a Save Britain Fund and even offered emergency food supplies. Unemployment was also rising and in January 1975 breached the psychological barrier of one million.

The events of 1976 that lead up to the sterling collapse can provide useful insights into the situation facing European economies in the early years of the 21st century: attempting to control public deficits while supporting demand. A lesson then, as now, was that material changes in policy may not arrive soon enough to placate the markets. The problems in Ireland, Greece, Spain and the UK, to name but a few, did not appear overnight but politicians, the financial press and economists were slow to conclude that previous policies were unsustainable and this was the same in 1976.

In the 1976 crisis the turning point in policy came as late as the beginning of 1975. As the then Chancellor, Denis Healey, wrote: "I abandoned

Keynesianism in 1975." As we saw with Ireland and Greece, action was forced on them as borrowing costs rose to extreme heights; and for Greece in particular borrowing was nearly impossible. A common trait of politicians both this century and the last is that they are loathe to admit to any crisis and so policy shifts are inevitably late in coming. Edmund Dell captured this speaking after the February 1974 election. He said: "Some ministers seemed unconscious of the economic crisis that had struck the country. Their attitude resembled that of characters in Jane Austen's novels who carried on their lives undisturbed by the Napoleonic Wars."

Crises tend to build on small events. In the 1976 crisis the cracks started to appear on 9 March 1976 when Nigeria announced its intention to diversify its foreign exchange reserves, which for historical reasons were heavily weighted towards sterling. The following day the Labour government lost a House of Commons vote on public expenditure cuts designed to win support from the IMF (the UK had made an application to the IMF for a standby facility). Despite winning a confidence vote on 11 March 1976 the Prime Minister decided to resign a few days later on 16 March. Sterling was now on the run despite intervention, and interest rates reached 15% on 6 October. The scale of the sterling collapse was immense. GBP/USD fell from above 2.40 in April 1975 to just below 1.60 in November 1976 and GBP/DEM (Deutschmark) from 6.10 to around 3.90 over the same period.

On 7 June the UK announced a $5.3bn six-month credit facility from other central banks, $2bn of which came from the US central bank. However, the US imposed a payment deadline of 9 December 1976. The UK was unable to meet this condition, which prompted the application to the IMF for a standby loan of $3.9bn on 29 September 1976. The US position was hardly supportive but has echoes of Germany today – they were unwilling to bail out a country with flawed economic policies. Cuts in UK public spending inevitably followed.

The notion that Ireland or Greece would have been saved by devaluation is an illusion. Their debt levels were extremely high and their ability to borrow extremely low. As was graphically seen in 1976, a falling currency severely impacts on inflation and any flexibility on domestic monetary policy.

1980s

The impact of the current account and interest rates on the exchange rate was never so clearly demonstrated as from 1978 to 1981. During this period sterling rose by over 20% against a basket of currencies. The arrival of North Sea oil in 1976, coupled with the second oil crisis of 1978-79, had turned a traditional deficit on the oil account into a substantial surplus; sterling was now viewed as a petro-currency. At the same time the UK was experiencing a boom, which, despite the oil surplus, contributed to a deficit in the current account that was countered by a sharp rise in interest rates attracting speculative flows.

From 1978 to 1980 the bank interest rate rose from 6.5% to 17%. This inevitably led to a sharp fall in manufacturing production and imports, which led to record surplus in 1981. Two factors mitigated against even greater sterling gains: the abolition of exchange controls in November 1979, which prompted large investment outflows, and Bank of England intervention. By 1981 sterling started to ease back but the damage had been done and British manufacturing had been dealt a blow it would never recover from.

The European Union at this time was looking for greater political and monetary union and in 1979 the European Monetary System (EMS) was established. The most important component of this system was the Exchange Rate Mechanism (ERM). Member countries agreed to peg currencies within a 2.25% band of a weighted average of European currencies; this weighted average was called the European Currency Unit (ECU). The early period was characterised by regular re-alignments – from 1979 to 1987 there were 11. The usual pattern was for low inflation, low surplus countries such as Germany and Holland to revalue and for high inflation, high deficit countries such as France and Italy to devalue. This arrangement is known as a 'currency bloc': a group of currencies fixed in value against one another but floating against all others.

During the 1980s the primary UK policy objective was the control of inflation through essentially the targeting of money supply growth. This met with mixed results and it was felt by Chancellor Lawson by the mid-1980s that joining the ERM would impose a low inflation discipline. Prime Minister Thatcher refused but nonetheless the Chancellor pursued a policy of shadowing the Deutschmark, a beacon of post-war low inflationary growth. However, this coincided with strong economic growth, popularly known as the Lawson boom. In 1986 the current account deficit was £2.3bn, by 1988 this had risen to £17.5bn and inflation was on the rise despite tagging the Deutschmark (DM).The exchange rate policy was abandoned and interest rates were raised from 7.5% in May 1988 to 15% in October 1989, providing support to the pound.

While the deficit started to contract inflation was stubborn and in September 1990, with a view to further deflating the economy, the UK joined the ERM at DM 3 to the pound. Even at the time this was considered too high an exchange rate. By 1991 inflation started to fall and the UK economy was in recession. UK inflation was still high relative to its main trading partners and sterling was unable to devalue sufficiently to restore competitiveness because of ERM membership. By 1992 the current account deficit had increased to £10.1bn, a remarkable level given the scale of the recession. The government wanted to cut rates but sterling was trading close to the lower end of its trading band within the ERM. An exit from the ERM and an ensuing devaluation was discounted on fears of reviving inflation. There was also a considerable amount of political capital invested in staying within the system.

1990s

In July and August 1992 sterling came under intense selling pressure, which prompted the Bank of England to intervene to keep sterling above the lower band. The most famous seller was George Soros. On 15 September, Black Wednesday, interest rates were raised to 15% but the selling continued and Chancellor Norman Lamont was forced to announce that the UK was leaving the ERM the next day. The pound fell 10% immediately. The scale of intervention is not known but it ran into billions. It is believed that no losses were incurred. These transactions were turned for a profit in later years.

The importance of these events cannot be overstated. If sterling had weathered this attack it probably would have entered the euro in 1999. Instead, it reinforced the euro sceptic camp and floating rate advocates. The UK would not again attempt to control the value of sterling. For the Conservative government it was a total disaster and arguably resulted in the party losing its reputation for financial soundness on the dealing room floor.

What the devaluation did achieve was to ignite a strong recovery in the economy and an improvement in the current account. From 1993 to 1997 a deficit of £10.6bn was transformed to a surplus of £6.6bn. More importantly, inflation did not erupt as the world economy was experiencing deflationary pressures. In 1996 sterling was again on the rise backed by high interest rates, relatively strong economic growth and subdued inflation.

2000s

The early years of 2000 were similarly characterised, although sterling found additional support from the rapid growth in financial services, which the UK dominated with the US, and the diversification of foreign exchange reserves by the world's central bank from dollars.

During this period the UK ran deficits on the current account but these were no longer an explicit policy constraint as they were viewed as self-correcting in the long run and in a period of global monetary expansion foreign investors were prepared to finance it. This all came to a sorry end in 2008 when the global financial system, in particular in the UK, imploded. The markets reverted to risk aversion with massive flows into safe-haven assets such as US Treasuries and out of deficit currencies and emerging market equities (risk assets). Sterling capitulated as huge borrowings in low interest currencies, notably the yen and Swiss franc (CHF) (carry trades), were unwound and investors sold sterling as more bank losses and failures were revealed.

2.

CENTRAL BANKS AND FOREIGN EXCHANGE INTERVENTION

WHAT IS FOREIGN EXCHANGE INTERVENTION?

Foreign exchange *intervention* is often quoted in the news but rarely will you see any working definition. I shall view it as any transaction or announcement by an official agent of a government that is intended to influence an exchange rate. Typically intervention operations are implemented by the monetary authority. Central banks tend to use a narrower definition, which is the sale or purchase of foreign currency against domestic currency in the foreign exchange market.

Intervention is normally transacted directly through the large commercial banks (normally of the country in question) and can be public or secret. It can be enacted through one bank or a number of banks to achieve maximum impact or visibility. Secret interventions are difficult to hide and sometimes may be carried out by the Bank for International Settlements.

The problem central banks face is the market perception that they have set an exchange rate level to protect (commonly referred to as a line in the sand). This invariably tempts the market to test resolve and pockets of the central bank by continuing to buy or sell.

During the period in which countries followed the Bretton Woods 'exchange rate system' intervention operations were required whenever rates exceeded their parity bands. After the breakdown of the system in 1973 intervention was left to the discretion of individual countries. It was not until 1977 that the IMF provided its member countries three principles to adhere to in their intervention policy.[3] The principles said that countries should:

1. not manipulate exchange rates in order to prevent balance of payments adjustment or to gain unfair competitive advantage over others

2. intervene to counter disorderly market conditions

3. take into account the exchange rate interests of others.

These principles implicitly assume that intervention policy can influence exchange rates.

---

[3] IMF Board Decision No 5392-(77 63), adopted April 1977.

The US was actively involved in intervention during the 1970s but was absent from 1981 through 1984. However, in early 1985 after the dollar had appreciated by over 40% and the US trade deficit was approaching $100bn, the Federal Reserve (Fed) in the US joined with the German Bundesbank (BUBA) and the Bank of Japan (BoJ) to intervene against the dollar. In the autumn of 1985 the US and the rest of the G-5 (Germany, Japan, France and the UK) engaged in a number of large and coordinated operations as part of the Plaza Agreement. While the scale of central bank intervention was large in the post-1985 period relative to previous history, it was still small in relation to the overall market. The Plaza Agreement stated:

> "In view of the present and prospective changes in fundamentals some orderly appreciation of the main non-dollar currencies against the dollar is desirable. The Minister and Governors stand ready to cooperate more closely to encourage this when to do so would be helpful."[4]

During the period 1985-1987 the dollar fell by over 50% against the Deutschmark. Throughout the period the central banks' stated intention was to affect the level rather than the variability of exchange rates. However, in February 1987 the G-7 produced the Louvre Accord which stated that nominal exchange rates were "broadly consistent with underlying economic fundamentals" and should be stabilised at their current levels.[5]

Sterilised and unsterilised intervention

Intervention can be distinguished by whether it is sterilised or unsterilised; i.e., intervention that respectively does not or does change the monetary base (or money supply as an approximation). When a monetary authority buys (sells) foreign exchange its own monetary base increases (decreases) by the amount of the purchase (sale). If the authority wishes to reverse the effect on the domestic monetary base – sterilise – they would buy (sell) domestic bonds. Fully sterilised intervention does not directly affect prices or interest rates and so does not influence the exchange rate through these variables as ordinary monetary policy does.

---

[4] G-5, 22 September 1985.
[5] G-7, 22 February 1987.

Unsterilised intervention is effectively another way of conducting monetary policy; in other words it will affect the level of the exchange rate in proportion to the change in the relative supplies of domestic and foreign money. A currency swap can be used to sterilise an intervention. A swap is a transaction where a foreign currency is bought in the spot market and simultaneously sold in the forward market. A swap will have little affect on the exchange rate. In this process the spot leg of the swap is transacted in the opposite direction to the spot market intervention, leaving the forward leg intact.

How intervention is carried out

The forward market has been used on a number of occasions for intervention purposes. This is the purchase or sale of foreign exchange for delivery at a future date. Intervention in the forward market has the advantage that there is no immediate cash outlay and therefore the impact on domestic liquidity (and the need for sterilisation) is at least delayed until the maturity of the foreign exchange contracts. Public reports indicated that the Bank of Thailand used this to defend the baht in 1997 (Moreno 1997).

Options have been used in a few cases (such as in Mexico in August 1996) to intervene in the exchange market, but not recently. As is the case with forwards, options do not immediately change the level of reserves and therefore do not require sterilisation. However, in so far as intervention operates through signalling the intentions of central banks, transactions involving options may not quite have the desired visible impact. The spot market is the favoured vehicle.

INTERVENTION AND MONETARY POLICY

The impact of floating exchange rates on monetary policy (the process by which the monetary authority of a country controls the supply of money) has changed over the years. Initially monetary policy under floating exchange rates was characterised by targeting money growth. Interest rates were set to limit growth in monetary aggregates, which was viewed as the key to price stability. Since the exchange rate was not an explicit part of this strategy, foreign exchange interventions were not required.

The arrival of inflation targeting in the 1990s significantly challenged the one-variable approach; instead, all variables that might influence future inflation were taken into account in setting monetary policy. In this context the degree of exchange rate pass-through to domestic prices determines the extent to which the central bank will have to incorporate exchange rate movements in their decision process. If the exchange rate is important for future inflation (i.e., the pass-through effects of exchange rate changes on inflation occur faster than the interest rate effects on inflation) then it follows that intervention might be a useful instrument.

How monetary policy is conducted

Monetary policy can operate through monetary targeting, exchange rate targeting or inflation targeting. A *monetary targeting* strategy will have an implicit inflation target, which is used to determine the optimal growth of the monetary aggregate. Central banks that pursue *exchange rate targeting* do not require a target rate for inflation. Ideally, the exchange rate would be pegged to a low inflation currency with the aim of mirroring their inflation performance; as such there is no need to specify an inflation target rate.

This is quite the opposite of *inflation targeting*, where there is a specific figure announced and widely communicated. In this case there is no interim target for the public to observe, which of course raises the profile of the final target. Practically, all three strategies are managed through short-term interest rates.

A recent approach has been to take account of all indicators, known as a *look at everything* strategy, rather than a single variable. This is very much allied to improved communications (signalling) between the policy makers and the public, and genuine accountability. In the UK this is seen in the letter that is sent from the Bank of England Governor to the Chancellor if inflation deviates over 1% from target.

One common feature in this transparent approach is the publication of minutes of monetary meetings, albeit with a time lag. It is important that the public believe in the policy makers' commitment; anchoring inflation expectations is viewed as critical by all central bankers in public utterances and in official reports. The implicit assumption in inflation targeting is that low and stable inflation will promote macroeconomic goals such as economic growth and employment. Inflation targets are generally around 2% and are either published as a single figure or as a target range.

Events of 2008 and 2009 highlighted that monetary policy is not exclusively about preventing excessive inflation; many central banks at this time were looking to counter deflationary pressures (a decline in prices and weak growth) and in some cases sold their currency. Another good example of this is the Japanese policy response in 2001 to a decade long period of near zero growth and deflation. The policy conclusion was that the key to recovery was an expansion of the money supply. This was started in March 2001 by the adoption of quantitative easing (a term which has come into the public domain following the 2007-09 financial crisis). This was followed up by massive unsterilised intervention from the end of 2002 to 16 March 2004. To give some idea of the scale of intervention, on 5 March 2004 the Japanese purchased USD 11.2bn and sold yen.

By the end of 2003 there were signs of Japanese economic recovery and in March 2004 Alan Greenspan, the US Federal Reserve Bank Chairman, indicated that the intervention strategy had worked. He said:

> "Partially unsterilised intervention is perceived as a means of expanding the monetary base of Japan, a basic element of monetary policy. In time, however, as the present deflationary situation abates, the monetary consequences of continued intervention could become problematic. The current performance of the Japanese economy suggests that we are getting closer to the point where continued intervention at the present scale will no longer meet the monetary policy needs of Japan."

It should be noted that intervention had the full support of the US administration, which felt that economic stagnation was not in the interests of the US.[6] By not registering objections to the intervention the US effectively made it possible for the Japanese to operate in the market.

THE EFFICACY OF INTERVENTION

The effects of sterilised intervention are somewhat debatable. The standard approach is to view the potential impact through two routes: *the portfolio channel* and *the signalling channel*. In the former an intervention that changes the relative outstanding supply of assets denominated in domestic and foreign currencies will require a change in expected relative returns on the asset whose outstanding stock has increased, thereby leading to a change in the

---

[6] Taylor, 2006.

exchange rate. This is based on the assumption that investors consider foreign and domestic assets to be imperfect substitutes. The portfolio channel approach no longer carries much weight because the scale of possible intervention has declined relative to the size of the foreign exchange market. It may, however, have greater relevance in emerging markets where central bank reserve holdings are large relative to local market turnover.

It is widely thought that intervention operates mainly through *the signalling channel*. This may convey to the market future changes in monetary or exchange rate policy or that the authorities view the exchange rate to be out of line with economic fundamentals. A sterilised purchase (sale) of domestic currency reflects a desire for a stronger (weaker) domestic currency and this desire eventually leads to a tighter (looser) monetary policy. However, monetary policy may cause the exchange rate to appreciate or depreciate too much and prompts intervention to moderate or even reverse the trend of exchange rate movements. Dealers' reactions (and success) will much depend on the perceived credibility of the central bank.

A signal may be used to reduce market expectations of current and future volatility. In recent years this has been the dominant theme – to reduce excessive exchange rate volatility. That being said, central banks may desire an increase in short-term volatility if they are faced with an undesirable exchange rate trend. The central bank will attempt to remove or reduce the one-way bet mentality by restoring two-way risk. Signalling intentions can of course be made clear via verbal commentaries, or 'jawboning' as it is described in the market.

There is secret intervention which fits neither the portfolio channel nor the signalling channel. By definition it is virtually impossible to get a handle on this. It is difficult to see this changing a trend but it may well slow down the process, providing a two-way risk dimension.

One way that intervention can be made more visible is through concerted efforts and this can indicate a strong commitment to exchange rate changes. The difficulty arises when too many central banks get involved. The market loses faith in the message in so far as a wide range of countries with skewed economic fundamentals may indicate a different policy requirement.

Coordinated intervention, however, is rare. A recent case of coordinated intervention was on 18 March 2011 when the Japanese were joined by the Group of Seven (G7) major industrialised countries to stall the surge in the yen after the tsunami and nuclear incident in Japan prompted market chaos. The G7 statement said that this action was to stabilise "excess volatility" and "disorderly movements in exchange rates". The last previous coordinated intervention was in 2000 when the euro was bought.

Models of exchange rate behaviour assume that currency prices are efficient aggregators of information and market expectations are rational. In practice the foreign exchange markets may not be efficient and intervention signals may not always be credible or unambiguous. The question of whether intervention policy influences exchange rate volatility obviously depends on the definition of 'volatility'. According to Dominguez and Frankel (1993) unanticipated and coordinated interventions are most effective. When there is high frequency of intervention the market has become too familiar and the impact is reduced.

Studies on the Japanese experience by Fatum and Hutchison, and Ito, revealed that intervention tends to be effective during a period of infrequent interventions (1999 to 2002) but ineffective (2003) or counterproductive during a period of very frequent interventions (first quarter 2004). An and Sun suggest that there is no uniform answer as to whether it is monetary policy or foreign exchange intervention which is more influential on exchange rates.

The importance of the policies on exchange rate fluctuations are country-specific; i.e., in some countries policy might effect the exchange rate to a similar degree as foreign exchange intervention while in other countries the impact of intervention might be much stronger. It is no great surprise therefore that Kim (2003) finds that foreign exchange interventions have a much greater impact on the exchange rate in the US as they do not target the exchange rate and interventions are infrequent.

Recessions and intervention – the case of the Swiss franc

Exchange rates become increasingly important in recessions as governments (in the absence of inflation constraints) look to combat deflationary pressures by promoting a weak currency. An insight to this thinking comes from the statement from Thomas Jordan, member of the Governing Board of the Swiss National Bank on 25 the September 2009:

> The Swiss franc plays a key role in the development of the Swiss economy. Through the competitiveness of our export pricing, it

impacts on our exports and consequently affects the business cycle. Via import prices, it has a direct impact on consumer prices. In addition, the Swiss franc has been – and still is – a factor in the success of the Swiss financial sector. The Swiss National Bank (SNB) takes the exchange rate into account in its monetary policy although it does not normally exert any direct influence on it. In the past, it has only been in rare emergency situations that the SNB intervened to directly influence exchange rate developments. However, from March 2009, the appreciation of the Swiss franc induced by safe haven effects, in an exceptionally difficult economic situation entailing deflation risks, prompted the SNB to prevent an appreciation of the Swiss franc against the euro by purchasing foreign currency.

For Switzerland, trade with the EU is very important to the economy. Exports to the EU as a percentage of total exports are 60%, while exports to the EU as a percentage of GDP are 23%. Therefore, the level of EUR/CHF is critical.

In 2009 and 2010 ongoing weakness of the euro and the reinstatement of the Swiss franc as a primary safe haven currency prompted action on a number of occasions. On 12 March 2009 the SNB bought at 1.4790 to move the price to 1.5340. This price movement can be seen in Figure 2.1.

Figure 2.1 – SNB buying CHF to move it from 1.4790 to 1.5340 against the euro

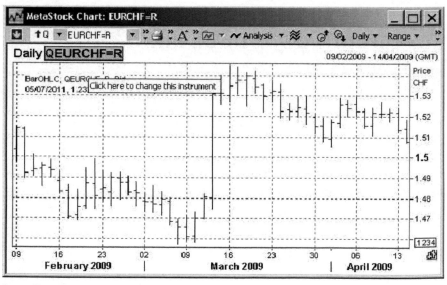

Source: Reuters

On 24 June 2009 the SNB bought and moved the CHF rate from 1.5020 to 1.5380 against the euro, which can be seen in Figure 2.2.

Figure 2.2 – SNB buys CHF to move it from 1.5020 to 1.5380 against the euro

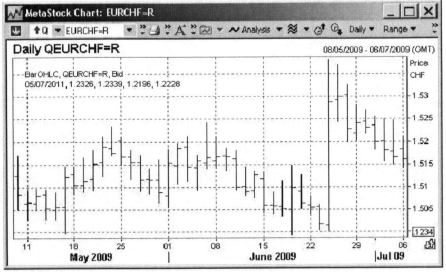

Source: Reuters

It could be argued that the Swiss intervention was an outright failure. The authorities were forced to stand aside against the weight of Swiss franc buying and by August 2011 EUR/CHF had touched 1.05. In the same month the Swiss authorities adopted a zero interest rate policy to deter inflows.

CONCLUSION

This topic is very broad and while we can see that the role of intervention has generated a lot of debate and research amongst the academic community, the results are not clear cut. This, however, has not deterred a number of monetary authorities from intervening with some frequency. This has been particularly evident in Asia.

The importance to the market is that intervention does influence exchange rates and hedging policy. The difficulty for the market lies in determining the degree of impact and its sustainability.

3.

THE BASICS OF FOREIGN EXCHANGE

A DEFINITION OF FOREIGN EXCHANGE

All claims on foreign currency payable abroad, whether consisting of funds in foreign currency held with banks abroad, or bills or cheques, again in foreign currency and payable abroad, are foreign exchange (also called Forex or FX). In the trading of foreign exchange between banks only foreign currency held with banks abroad is concerned. For the purposes of this book foreign exchange only applies to bank balances denominated in foreign currency.

Foreign bank notes are not foreign exchange in this sense. They can be converted into foreign exchange provided they can be placed without restriction to the credit of an ordinary commercial account abroad. A currency, whether in foreign exchange or bank notes, is deemed convertible if the person holding it can convert (exchange) it freely into any other currency. Convertibility may be unrestricted or partial. Sterling, since 1979, is fully convertible whether the holder is resident in the UK or abroad, and regardless of whether it is a matter of current payments or financial transactions. Some countries recognise only external or non-resident convertibility.

Regulations may also draw a distinction, as far as convertibility is concerned, between funds arising from current transactions (goods and services) and those coming from purely financial operations. Exchange controls were common in the West until the 1980s. They now tend to be operated in emerging countries, especially in Asia and the Far East. It is important to ascertain prior to any transactions what conditions apply. It is usually easy to invest into a country but can prove extremely difficult to repatriate.

THE FOREIGN EXCHANGE MARKET

The foreign exchange market is not a physical place. It operates on a global basis through a computer-linked group of banks whose function is to facilitate trading by providing buying and selling prices to the main participants (these are noted below). This is known as an over-the-counter (OTC) market. Banks are the intermediary between foreign exchange supply and demand. The interbank market is the wholesale market and this is where the banks trade with one another.

The development in communications and dealing technology has meant that there is a uniform price for a particular currency throughout the financial centres of the world. The main centres of trading are London and New York. Trading is continual from Sunday evening 20.00 GMT to Friday evening 22.00 GMT.

Historically, transactions would occur over the phone, telex or via brokers but now dealing platforms and electronic broking systems dominate, for example EBS. According to the BIS (Bank for International Settlements) Triennial central bank Survey 2010, the foreign exchange market turnover is about $4trn a day, which makes it the largest, most liquid financial market in the world.

These characteristics of the foreign exchange market – high liquidity, 24-hour trading and price fluctuation – are attractive to speculators and this explains why this market has become the largest in the world.

Currency pairs and ISO abbreviations

In the market, abbreviations are used to refer to the various currencies. These can be represented by commonly used symbols or three letter codes as set by the International Organization for Standardization (ISO). The following ISO codes are used in this book:

- pound sterling (GBP)

- US dollar (USD)

- euro (EUR)

- Swiss franc (CHF)

- Japanese yen (JPY)

This group of currencies are generally referred to as the *majors*, based quite simply on the volumes transacted. The Australian dollar (AUD) is sometimes also included, although it normally comes under the *commodity* currency umbrella which includes Canada (CAD), New Zealand (NZD), South Africa (ZAR) and Norway (NOK).

In foreign exchange two currencies are always involved. The rate of exchange is the price of one currency in terms of another. For example, the relation of British pounds to US dollars will be shown as GBP/USD.

The size, scope and growth of the foreign exchange market

Market share by country

The foreign exchange market share by country can be seen in Table 3.1.

Table 3.1 – Foreign exchange market share by country in 2007 and 2010

Country	2007 market share (%)	2010 market share (%)
United Kingdom	35	37
USA	17	18
Euro-zone	11	9
Japan	6	6
Switzerland	6	5

The UK dominates foreign exchange trading, with a market share of 37% in 2010 (up from 35% in 2007). The growth in the UK becomes even more stark when compared with 1995 when its market share was 29%. The euro-zone's market share has virtually halved since 1995 and now accounts for just 9%. The US accounted for 18% in 2010, which is broadly in line with the past ten years' experience. The US is followed by Japan on 6%.

The other main trading centres, Singapore, Switzerland and Hong Kong, account for around 5% each with Australia accounting for 4%. A notable loser in recent years has been Japan, which has seen its share collapse from 10% in 1995, possibly reflecting a stagnant economy and banking problems.

Growth of foreign exchange trading

The pace of growth in foreign exchange trading has slowed in recent years, but the numbers are nonetheless impressive. Looking at the data in Table 3.2, the top row – Foreign exchange instruments – shows that overall turnover in the world markets in 2010 was up 18% on 2007 and over 300% since 2001. The growth was largely driven by spot transactions, which were up 48%, and by outright forwards, which increased by 31% from 2007 to 2010. These are referred to in the market as *plain vanilla* transactions by virtue of their simplicity.

Table 3.2 – Global foreign exchange market turnover by instrument

Average daily turnover (USD bn)	1998	2001	2004	2007	2010
Foreign exchange instruments	1527	1239	1934	3324	3981
Spot transactions	568	386	631	1005	1490
Outright forwards	128	130	209	362	475
Foreign exchange swaps	734	656	954	1714	1765
Currency swaps	10	7	21	31	43
Options and other products	87	60	119	212	207

Source: BIS (Bank for International Settlements)

The figures show that spot trades account for 37% of transactions, which is similar to 1998 levels and up from 30% in 2007. This particular situation may be a result of the 2007-09 financial crisis, as company boardrooms might have been less inclined to use more sophisticated instruments and looked to take a more conservative approach.

The use of options fell to USD 207bn per day in April 2010, from USD 212bn in 2007, although one should not lose sight of the rapid growth in the preceding decade. The most actively traded instrument remains foreign exchange swaps, which were almost unchanged from 2007 to 2010 with daily turnover of USD 1.8trn. This reflects the critical role of swaps in the hedging process, which I shall be covering later.

Market share by currency

The currency distribution of global foreign exchange turnover shown in Table 3.3 comes as no surprise. As befits its reserve currency status, the dollar remains the most traded currency, accounting for 85% of all transactions. The euro and the yen account for 39% and 19% respectively.

Table 3.3 – Most traded currencies by market share

Currency	Daily market share (%)
United States dollar (USD)	85
Euro (EUR)	39
Japanese yen (JPY)	19
Pound sterling (GBP)	13
Australian dollar (AUD)	8

Emerging market (EM) currencies are still traded in relatively small size, accounting between them for less than 20% of total transaction volume. Notable within this group are India, Korea, Taiwan and China. EM is an area of expected growth for the future, especially if China adopts a flexible exchange rate system for the renminbi (CNY). In the 2010 figures USD/CNY accounted for only 0.8% of daily turnover.

Market share by currency pair

If one looks at currency pairs by market share (Table 3.4), EUR/USD dominates, accounting for 28% of market share, which is USD 1.1trn per day, up from USD 372bn in 2001. Market share has been around this level for the past ten years. The share of USD/JPY is 14%, but this appears to be on a declining trend having accounted for 19% in 1998. GBP/USD comes in at 9%, a level which has been remarkably steady over the past decade and leaves sterling as the fourth most traded currency, followed by AUD, CHF and CAD.

Table 3.4 – Most traded currency pairs by market share

Currency pair	Market share 2010 (%)
EUR/USD	28
USD/JPY	14
GBP/USD	9
AUD/USD	6
USD/CAD	5

Who trades foreign exchange?

The following is a list of the groups that trade foreign exchange and their main purposes in doing so.

Corporates, commodity trading accounts (CTAs)

Transactions are driven by:

- payables
- receivables
- inter-company loans
- dividends
- royalties
- acquisitions
- divestitures.

Companies will need to record for accounting purposes the value of assets, liabilities and equity and reported income relating to overseas subsidiaries/investments. This is commonly referred to as 'translation' exposure. This exposure will be recorded in the financial statements as an exchange rate gain (or loss).

Portfolio fund managers

Transactions are driven by:

- sale and purchase of fixed income, equities and real estate of foreign denominated assets held within portfolio
- overall currency exposure which can be managed by outside currency manager.

Hedge funds

- Trade foreign exchange as a separate asset class
- Speculate using computer models
- Buy and sell foreign-denominated assets within the fund.

Central banks:

- maintain foreign currency reserves and will adjust weightings of currencies
- are responsible for inter-government and institutional settlements
- may intervene in the market to affect the value of the domestic currency.

Sovereign wealth funds (SWFs)

Sovereign wealth funds (SWFs) are state-owned investment funds. SWFs are focused on longer-term returns and can generally hold a wide range of currencies and assets, which translates to more diversification versus central bank reserve managers. About 66% of SWFs are largely funded by oil and gas exports while non-commodity SWFs are typically funded by transfer of assets from official foreign exchange reserves and government budget surpluses. Examples of major funds are Abu Dhabi (ADIA), Kuwait (KIA), Government Fund of Norway and the Chinese SAFE Investment Company.

Commercial banks

Spot trading

- interbank market making
- servicing client orders
- speculation.

Forward trading

- interbank market making
- speculation
- works with money market desk to manage bank's balance sheet funding.

Option trading

- interbank market making
- speculation.

Private individuals

- speculation
- sale and purchase of overseas assets – usually property
- hedging currency exposures.

Banks' share of global foreign exchange

Over the past 25 years a combination of large bank mergers and aggressive trading practices has effectively muscled the small banks out of the foreign exchange market, although traditionally they had supported it. It is now estimated that the top ten banks account for over 75% of foreign exchange transactions by volume and the top five somewhere from 50% to 60%.

Trading is increasingly being done over electronic platforms (e-trading) and this means that concentration becomes even more pronounced, with the top three platforms (Deutsche, Barclays, UBS) estimated to account for around 60% of the business. Indeed, the banks' focus is on enhancing electronic trading platforms to attract the customer. It has taken a long time and considerable expense from the big players to build up this infrastructure. This creates huge entry barriers or at best a serious challenge for aspiring new entrants.

These multi-dealer trading venues are commonly referred to as electronic communication networks (ECNs) and formed the second phase of the electronic revolution led by Reuters and EBS with electronic inter-dealer brokers in the mid-1990s. EBS and Reuters Match are still the primary funnel for foreign exchange business.

The major banks' emphasis is in fact not so much trading in a proprietary manner but to attract transactional and trading flows, i.e., volume. Foreign exchange is considered a core product for the major banks. There is very little capital required to support the business, which is essentially an off balance sheet product.

Furthermore, the product is for the most part short-dated, extremely liquid and client-driven, which adds to its attractions. This in turn generates an impressive return on capital. It is generally recognised that for banks to offer a full service, scale is required; first, to provide liquidity and, second, value- added services, such as technical research, that differentiate them from the pack.

It should be emphasised that the key issue is not so much about price, as, for the vast majority of time, there is not much difference in this respect amongst the major banks. It has more to do with the provision of liquidity to their customers. This boils down to the willingness and ability to quote prices in virtually all conditions and in the required size.

Foreign exchange, however, is still relationship-based and while customers use e-commerce tools (dealing platforms) in volatile markets, ideas (market colour) can only be provided direct from the dealing room. This is invaluable.

The BIS figures in Table 3.2 show that the foreign exchange market continues to grow. It is without doubt the largest and most liquid market available, and is likely to be spared undue regulation in the future, unlike derivatives. It is apparent, however, that liquidity, if we take turnover as a proxy, is limited to a small group of currencies and is concentrated within a very small number of banks. I shall be talking more about liquidity later, in chapter 11.

The underlying message of this book is that with floating exchange rates comes extreme volatility and with that comes an increasing need to hedge or manage that volatility. The data we looked at above (again, in Table 3.2) suggest that hedging is indeed increasingly employed, with vanilla products (spot and forwards) still the favoured method. I will discuss these vanilla products in depth for this very reason.

The growth of sovereign wealth funds, hedge funds and international funds in general has certainly driven foreign exchange activity for portfolio diversification and trading. The foreign exchange market is probably going to be a larger focus for investors in the years ahead given all of the above and because increasing government debt issuance globally will require some element of overseas buyers.

4.

THE THEORY OF FOREIGN EXCHANGE: HOW EXCHANGE RATES ARE DETERMINED

The exchange rate is the price at which one currency is convertible into another, for example an exchange rate of 1.7000 for GBP/USD means £1 will buy $1.70. Exchange rates relate prices and costs in one economy to those in other economies.

The rate can be set in various ways. It may be fixed by the government, laid out in an international treaty, or it could be linked to something external, for example gold. However, most exchange rates are defined by a floating exchange rate system, as discussed in chapter 1. Thus the following chapter applies to a floating exchange rate system.

EXCHANGE RATES AND SUPPLY AND DEMAND

In a floating exchange rate system, the price of a currency is determined in the same way as any price – by supply and demand. Figure 4.1 illustrates the supply and demand curves for pounds traded against US dollars on the foreign exchange market.

The *demand curve* is assumed to be downward sloping (as it is for all goods). If the price of the pound falls against the dollar then the price of UK goods will fall in dollar terms. For example, if the exchange rate falls from £1=$2 to £1=$1 then a UK good costing £2000 will fall in price for the US from $4000 to $2000. The US should therefore buy more UK goods and demand more pounds to pay for them.

The *supply curve* is upward sloping because a fall in the value of the pound will increase the price of foreign imports for the UK leading them to reduce their purchases of foreign goods and in turn foreign exchange. Where supply is equal to demand – an exchange rate of 1.7000 in Figure 4.1 – this is termed the 'equilibrium exchange rate'.

Figure 4.1 – The supply and demand of pounds traded on the foreign exchange market

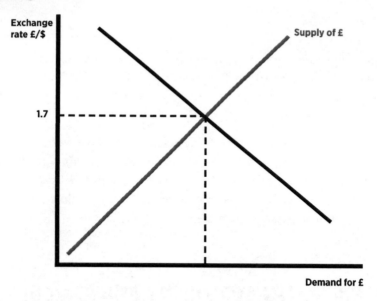

When the exchange rate for a country's currency in terms of another currency rises we say that the country's currency has *appreciated*. For instance, if the exchange rate rises from £1:$1 to £1:$2 it is said that sterling has appreciated against the dollar (the dollar has depreciated against sterling). Each pound will now purchase more dollars. When the exchange rate falls, for instance from £1:$2 to £1:$1, we can say sterling has *depreciated* against the dollar (the dollar has appreciated against sterling).

In very simple terms, if a currency is expected to appreciate then demand for that currency will increase, and if a currency is expected to depreciate, demand for that currency will fall.

The demand for pounds comes from people who are investing in the UK from abroad, or from firms who are buying UK exports, that need pounds to pay for the goods. The supply of pounds comes from people in the UK or foreign investors who are selling pounds. This may be because they have bought goods from overseas (imports), or it may simply be that they are investing in another country and so need the local currency. To get this they have to sell pounds in exchange for the other currency. The demand and supply functions are constantly changing with exchange rate expectations and interest rate differentials.

The theoretical rationale for downward sloping demand curves and upward sloping supply curves essentially rests on assumptions about the buying and selling of currency for exports and imports. With regard to long-term capital flows, for instance buildings, land and companies, it is not clear how buyers and sellers react to rises and falls in the price of the currency and these assumptions are unlikely to strictly apply. Nonetheless, the supply and demand function gives us a very useful tool for analysing movements in the exchange rate.

Example – the Bank of England increases interest rates

Let us take an example where UK interest rates are increased by the Bank of England. This will tend to attract short-term money flows, which are encouraged by relative real interest rate advantage (a real interest rate advantage means the rate has been adjusted for inflation). To invest, pounds have to be bought and so the demand for pounds will rise. This situation is illustrated in Figure 4.2, where there is a shift in the demand curve from D1 to D2.

Figure 4.2 – A shift in the demand curve as the demand for pounds rises

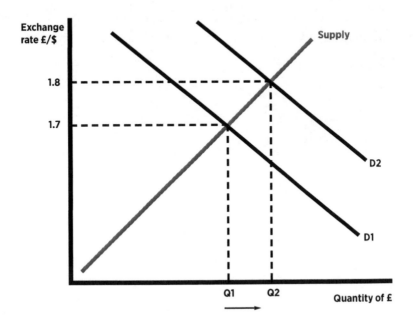

Figure 4.2 shows a situation where both the exchange rate and the volume of currency traded have increased. This will not inevitably be the case, as there may be other factors affecting the exchange rate at the same time. A lot will also depend on whether the foreign exchange market expected the Bank of England to make the interest rate increase.

Central banks, governments, and supply and demand

We have already discussed the role of central banks in the foreign exchange market in chapter 2. Looking at Figure 4.2 we can see, at least in theory, how the Bank of England can act on behalf of the government to influence the exchange rate. They have, though, not done this since the ERM crisis of 1992, however.

If they want to intervene in this way, the government will need to use their foreign exchange reserves. They will need to buy or sell foreign currency as appropriate to try to influence the market. Say, for example, that the exchange rate has been depreciating for some time (people have been selling the pound) and the government wants to try to slow its fall (or even reverse it). The government will need to increase the level of demand for the pound, and they do this by buying sterling and selling other currencies.

Figure 4.3 shows how this would affect the supply curve. The selling of sterling pushes the supply curve to the right (S1 to S2) and forces the exchange rate down.

Figure 4.3 – Sale of sterling forces the exchange rate down

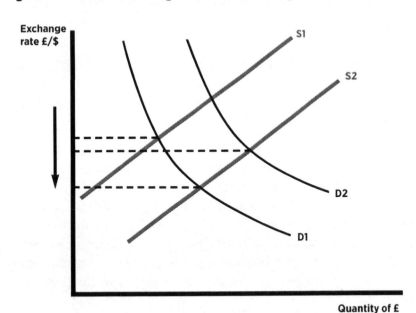

The government decides to act, and so they sell dollars and buy sterling in exchange. This increases the demand for sterling, and pushes the demand curve to D2. The pound has still fallen overall, but the government's action has slowed the fall.

If the opposite was happening and sterling was rising the government would need to buy foreign currency and sell sterling. This would increase the supply of sterling and help to slow down the appreciation.

THE EFFECT OF EXCHANGE RATES ON AN ECONOMY

Exchange rate changes can have a significant effect on the economy. Let's take the example of a depreciation of the exchange rate, and see what impact this has. If the exchange rate falls, this changes the relative prices of imports and exports. Exports will appear relatively cheap in other currencies, and imports will appear expensive.

Rising input costs will eventually filter into the finished product and into the consumer price index (CPI – the standard measure of inflation produced by measuring the changes in prices of a basket of goods and services), meaning that the costs of everyday goods will increase. There we have the first effect of a depreciation – it could trigger inflationary pressures in the economy. Assuming demand for exports increases and the demand for imports falls this will have a positive effect on overall demand which may compound this inflationary impact if the economy is close to productive capacity.

In the long run the effect of the depreciation on the balance of payments is far from certain. The impact depends on how sensitive the demand for imports and exports is to the changes in the prices of these products. This sensitivity is measured by the price elasticity of demand (PED) for imports and exports, which is calculated like so:

Price elasticity of demand (PED) = Percentage change in quantity demanded/Percentage change in price

In theory PED varies from zero (infinitely inelastic – there is no response in demand to a change in price) to infinity (infinitely elastic). Thefore a fall in price would lead to an infinite increase in quantity demanded and a rise in price would lead to the quantity demanded becoming zero. If the value of PED is greater than 1 it is elastic and if the value of PED is less than 1, it is inelastic. For instance, if an increase in price of 5% leads to a fall in quantity demanded of 10%, then the PED is 2. If an increase in price of 50% leads to a fall in quantity demanded of 25% then the PED is 0.5.

When the exchange rate falls, imports become more expensive and exports cheaper. That should raise the demand for exports and lower the demand for imports. However, although the exports are cheaper for those buying them abroad we still receive the same amount in sterling. Imports cost us more in sterling because although the price in the local currency is the same more pounds are needed to buy this local currency. The overall effect on the balance of payments depends on the price elasticity of exports and imports.

Some simple examples can be used to illustrate this point.

Price elasticity of demand examples

Assume the exchange rate between the pound and the euro is £1:€2. A product, X, in the UK, is priced at £5. At this exchange rate 100 of these items are purchased from abroad and export earnings are therefore £500 (100 x £5). A product, Y, in Europe is locally priced at €5. The UK buys 200 of these items at the current exchange rate. This means that the UK has to give up £2.50 (5/2) to buy each unit. Total expenditure on imports is therefore £500. At this point the balance of payments is 0.

Let us now assume that the exchange rate depreciates from £1:€2 to £1:€1. Europeans buying product X from the UK will now have to give up only €5 to acquire the good rather than the €10 they had to pay previously. Given that the product appears cheaper we would expect demand for exports to rise. UK buyers of product Y from Europe, however, now have to give up £5 to acquire the necessary euro to buy the product. It appears to the UK buyer that prices have risen and we would expect demand for imports to fall. The price of exports has fallen by 50% whilst the price of imports appears to have risen by 100%.

Now let us look at the impact on the actual demand for imports and exports given two different scenarios.

Scenario 1

The Price Elasticity of Demand (PED) for exports is -1.4 (elastic) and the PED for imports is -0.2. Demand for exports would rise by 1.4 times the fall in price and so would rise by 70 units (50 x 1.4). In this case, export earnings would now be 170 x £5 = £850. Demand for imports would fall by 0.2 times the change in price and so would fall by 20% (0.2 x 100), a decrease of 40 units. Expenditure on imports would now be 160 x £5 = £800. We would now have a balance of payments surplus of £50.

Scenario 2

The PED of exports is -0.8 (inelastic) and the PED for imports is -0.5. Demand for exports would rise by 0.8 times the change in price (0.8 x 50) = 40 units. Total export earnings would be 140 x £5 = £700. Demand for imports would fall by 0.5 x the change in price (100%) = 50%. Import expenditure would now be 100 x £5 = £500. In this situation the balance of payments would be in surplus at £200.

The Marshall-Lerner condition says that if the sum of the price elasticity for imports and exports is greater than 1, then the balance of payments will improve. The evidence for the UK suggests that the condition holds in the long run, but not in the short run. This will mean that when the exchange rate depreciates, the balance of payments will initially deteriorate, but in the long-run it will improve. This gives what is known as a J-curve effect. This effect is shown in Figure 4.4.

Figure 4.4 – The J-curve effect

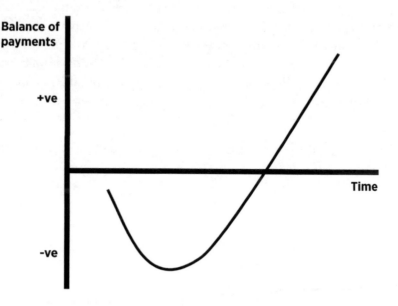

The J-curve effect occurs because it takes time for exchange rate changes to be factored in by decision makers – contracts will have previously been signed, for example, which will not immediately reflect any change in the exchange rate. The immediate impact therefore is not a quantity adjustment – more exports and fewer imports – but a price adjustment.

INTEREST RATE PARITY (IRP)

Foreign exchange theory has developed a framework to link spot and forward exchange rates, inflation and interest rates. This link is referred to as the interest rate parity (IRP) relation, and this can either be *covered* or *uncovered*. The difference between exchanging a currency now (the spot market) or at some point in the future (forward market) is clearly time. That time assumes a value which is the interest rate differential between the two currencies involved. The difference between the forward rate and the spot rate is called either a forward discount or forward premium. The IRP relationship is that the forward discount or premium equals the interest differential between the two currencies (net of transaction costs).

Covered IRP means that the currency exposure is hedged or covered by a forward contract. This process involves simultaneously borrowing currency A, converting it into currency B at the spot exchange rate, lending it and buying a forward contract to convert currency B into currency A at an agreed forward exchange rate. The net result of such a trade would be zero. Covered IRP holds because the market will trade away any anomalies, such as if forward premiums or discounts do not equate to interest rate differentials.

Uncovered IRP is when the exchange rate exposure is not protected by a forward contract. Uncovered IRP theory suggests that the expected change in the exchange rate will equal the interest rate differential. There is, however, no empirical evidence that the forward rate is a predictor of the future spot rate. If this was the case, futures contracts would not be bought because there would be no advantage in locking in a known forward rate with a forward contract – one would simply wait and transact at the future spot rate.

The usual technical explanation for the differential between the forward rate and the future spot rate is the existence of exchange risk premium, which is quite simply the compensation that risk-averse investors require for risk exposure. To look at it the other way round, the forward exchange rate discount or premium equals the expected exchange rate under the condition of no foreign currency risk premium.

PURCHASING POWER PARITY (PPP)

Exchange rate determination can also be viewed through the theory of purchasing power parity (PPP). There are two versions of PPP:

1.   absolute PPP (otherwise known as the law of one price),

2.   relative PPP.

1. Absolute PPP

Absolute PPP between any two countries is that amount of the currency of one country which endows the holder with the same amount of purchasing power – that is, command over goods and services as would a stated amount of the currency of the other country.[7]

Let's look at an example of this.

Let's assume that in the UK it takes £10 to buy a pair of jeans and in the US it takes $30. Therefore, if the rate of exchange between the UK and the US is 1:3 then PPP will exist, i.e., £1:$3. However, if the ratio moved to £1:$2 then it would become cheaper to purchase in one country as opposed to the other. If the exchange rate is £1:$2 then £10 equals only $20. So to obtain $30 you need £15 (£10 previously). The US is now more expensive and people would go to the UK to buy their jeans. This would increase demand for UK jeans leading the US to sell dollars and buy pounds. According to the PPP theory this would continue until the prices of the jeans in the UK equalled the prices in the US and parity was restored.

In practice no one would estimate the fundamental value of a currency by applying PPP to a single good. Some attempts have been made by incorporating a basket of goods, but goods consumed in different countries are rarely the same or they have different weightings. PPP is further undermined by distortions such as tariffs and transportation costs. PPP theory is a concept to be used for long-term analysis since under floating systems exchange rates tend to overshoot or undershoot long-term equilibrium rates, as indicated by PPP.

---

[7] Dr Gustav Cassel, 1916.

Therefore, PPP is not really used as a day-to-day trading tool; however, as a strategic guide it can have some use on the assumption that any deviation of the current exchange rate from this fundamental value (fair value) will be progressively corrected. In other words, PPP provides some indication of which direction prices should move in the medium term. In practice, analysts use a number of exchange rate models (including PPP), based on different economic approaches.

2. Relative PPP

A refinement on PPP (and the one normally referred to) is to take account of differences in inflation rates between countries. This is called relative PPP and states that changes in exchange rates should offset any inflation differential based on a basket of goods and services between the countries in question.

In simple terms, if Country A has a 3% inflation rate and Country B has a 1% inflation rate then Country A's currency should depreciate by 2% over the period. Simplicity, however, masks the issue of the inflation measure to be used and the base year. For instance, the consumer price index (CPI) has multiple interpretations and the inflation rate will depend on the basket of goods chosen for the index. As one example, there will be differences in price movements between tradable and non-tradable goods.

Intuitively this theoretical framework for exchange rate determination has attractions (the price level of a currency that is overvalued relative to its PPP is not sustainable) but again it has limited use in short-term foreign exchange trading.

If relative PPP theory holds, this has implications for asset managers, as exchange rate movements will have no relevance in their investment decisions. This is because exchange rate movements only reflect inflation differentials and will equalise real returns across countries. For example, take a UK asset with a 10% annual return, a UK inflation rate of 3% and a US inflation rate of 1.5%. If PPP holds, sterling will depreciate against the US dollar by approximately 1.5%. The US dollar return on the UK asset is approximately 10% - 1.5% = 8.5%. The real return for the UK and US investor is equal at about 7% (UK 10% - 3%, US 8.5% - 1.5%).

Another way to look at this concept is the proposition that exchange rates will adjust such that the return on investments with identical risk will be the same in any currency. The key element in this is expected exchange rates. Let's take, for example, Japanese interest rates as 1% (one year rate) and Australian interest rates as 4% (one year rate). A Japanese investor could sell yen and buy Australian dollars and gain 3% over one year. However, if the Australian dollar is expected to depreciate by 3% over this period there is no expected gain in investing in Australian dollars rather than yen. A 4% interest rate minus a 3% currency depreciation leaves a gain of 1%.

Irving Fisher stated in 1930 that real interest rates are equal across the world and stable over time. His underlying premise was that differences in real interest rates will not hold as capital flows take advantage of the differentials, which in turn will equalise real interest rates. As an approximation the real interest rate is the nominal (market) interest rate minus expected inflation. Movements in nominal interest rates are effectively driven by changes in inflationary expectations. In other words, the nominal interest rate differential between countries should be equal to the forecast inflation differential.

CURRENCIES OVERSHOOTING THEIR EXPECTED LEVELS — RUDIGER DORNBUSCH

In the opening chapter I suggested that life under a floating exchange rate system, while easing some of the immediate adjustment problems of the fixed rate system, came with its own baggage. The idea of the market determining the price had the approval of many illustrious conservative academics; it is difficult to argue in favour of exchange controls and other barriers to trade. However, prices under the floating system have been more volatile than many would have expected and at times have failed to reflect actual and expected interest rate differentials. What we have seen is currencies overshooting (or undershooting) on a regular basis.

In 1976 Rudiger Dornbusch addressed this issue in 'Expectations and Exchange Rate Dynamics', which was famously relabelled *the overshooting paper*. This was reviewed by K. Rogoff in his 2001 IMF lecture and I draw on his conclusions. Dornbusch showed that overshooting did not necessarily derive from market herd behaviour but from monetary shocks allied to rigidity in domestic prices and output. The core of his thinking was the uncovered interest parity condition and the money demand equation.

The *uncovered interest parity condition* states that if domestic and foreign bonds are perfect substitutes and capital is fully mobile across borders then the two bonds can only pay different interest rates if the market expects that there will be a compensating movement in the exchange rate. The key elements of the *money demand equation* are that the demand for money is proportional to the price level, an increase in output raises the transaction demand for money and higher interest rates lower the demand for money as the opportunity cost of holding money rises.

Dornbusch assumed that the domestic price level does not immediately move to an unanticipated monetary shock and that output also reacts slowly. So with an unanticipated rise in money supply and the price level temporarily sticky, the supply of real balances must rise. To establish an equilibrium, clearly the demand for real balances must also rise. With the assumption that output is fixed in the short run the only way that demand for real balances can go up is if the interest rate on domestic bonds falls. According to the uncovered interest rate parity condition, the interest rate can only fall if over the life of the bond the domestic currency appreciates to compensate. However, this runs at odds to the long-term view that a permanent increase in the money supply will generate a proportionate depreciation in the exchange rate. Dornbusch concluded that the initial depreciation of the exchange rate must be larger than the long-run depreciation. This initial excess depreciation overshoot leaves room for the appreciation required to bring equilibrium to the bond markets.

The Dornbusch approach is, if nothing else, elegant. In my view, no model or method has been yet devised that will consistently predict exchange rate movements under a floating rate system. Research suggests that the Dornbusch model will capture major turning points in monetary policy but it does not capture all of the other regular large swings we see.

This does not diminish Dornbusch's work; as Rogoff states: "the true strength of the model lies in that it highlights how one needs to think about the interaction of sluggishly adjusting goods markets and hyperactive asset markets." Overshooting is now in the public arena, regularly referred to by central bankers and mentioned in the press. Whether it can be considered a rational response to monetary shocks is still highly contentious.

5.

FOREIGN EXCHANGE IN PRACTICE

I n the opening chapters I have covered the history and theory of foreign exchange with a view to understanding the processes behind exchange rate determination. This forms an essential platform for a look at the practical issues in transacting foreign exchange, which is the core of the book.

In this chapter I shall be looking at the technical aspects of foreign exchange. This includes how foreign exchange prices are quoted. The concepts of different transactions – including spot, forward and swaps – and how they are calculated will be explained. At every opportunity I shall be applying this technical base to transactions that occur regularly.

PRICE QUOTATIONS

A rate of exchange is defined as the price of one currency in terms of another. It is either quoted for spot settlement or for future or forward delivery.

The party providing the price quote is called the market maker and the party asking for the price is called the market taker. In most circumstances the bank will be the market maker for customers.

In practice, whenever a bank is asked for a price two prices will be provided – the bid price and the offer price.

- *Bid* is the price at which the market maker buys the base currency (see below) and the market taker sells the base currency.

- *Offer* (known as the *ask* in the USA) is the price at which the market maker sells the base currency (see below) and the market taker buys the base currency.

Four typical examples of this are shown in Table 5.1.

Table 5.1 – Four examples of how bid/offer prices are displayed

Currency pair	Bid	Offer
GBP/USD	1.6515	1.6520
EUR/USD	1.3825	1.3830
USD/CHF	1.0535	1.0540
USD/JPY	91.20	91.25

Foreign exchange quotations are normally given with five digits. For example, EUR/USD 1.3825, GBP/USD 1.6515 or EUR/GBP 0.8805. USD/JPY would also be quoted to five digits when it is trading over 100, for example 110.25. When it is trading under 100, it is generally only quoted to four digits, for example 91.25. Electronic trading platforms do actually price to five decimal places and EUR/GBP is regularly quoted to five decimal places for large trades.

Base currency

Bid and offer prices are quoted in terms of the base currency. The base currency is always the first currency quoted and so in Table 5.1 the base currencies are sterling, euro and the dollar. The price quote you see tells you how many units of the other currency one unit of the base currency is equal to. Therefore, in the first row of the table, GBP 1 is equal to USD 1.6515. In the second row, EUR 1 is equal to USD 1.3825, and so on.

Market convention determines which currency will be the base. On its arrival in 1999 the euro became the base for all currency quotations in London. Even sterling had to give way and was quoted EUR 1 = so many pounds. At the inception of the euro the dealers in London actually started to quote GBP equal to so many EUR but the Bank of England quickly made it clear that the convention would be to quote the euro as the base.

The dollar is usually quoted as the base currency in pairs with other world currencies, reflecting its pre-eminence in world trade. Sterling is an exception, with dollars quoted as so many equal to one pound.

Knowing which currency is the base is important when one is establishing which currency is appreciating or depreciating. It is normal market practice to only talk in terms of the base currency appreciating or depreciating. Therefore, using the examples in Table 5.1:

If GBP/USD was quoted at 1.6515-20 and then moved to 1.6610-20, I would say sterling has appreciated against the dollar (one unit of sterling is now worth more dollars than it was before). The dollar in this case is depreciating. In the case of EUR/USD, if the price was quoted at 1.3825-30 and moved to 1.3725-30 the euro has depreciated against the dollar and the dollar has appreciated.

When asking for a spot price 'GBP/USD in 5', a professional dealer means that they want a price for the base currency – for GBP 5m. If they want a price in USD 5m this must be specified. Similarly, spot 'EUR/USD in 5' means EUR5m and 'USD/CHF in 5' means USD 5m (again, the base currencies are the reference point).

The word 'millions' would usually be omitted, talking in terms of 1, 2, 5, a pound or half a quid. A billion is called a yard and is very useful when dealing in Japanese yen.

Bid-offer spread

The difference between the bid and offer prices is called 'the spread'. Such a spread or turn is common to virtually all markets. It is clear that the choice of the rates favours the market maker or the one being asked to make a price, since when the market maker buys they buy at the lower (bid) price and when they sell, they sell at the higher (offer) price. As in all markets the trader wants to buy as low as possible and sell as high as possible. The dealing spread is the basis for profitable trading and is a key element in bank foreign exchange business models. For example:

Using rates from Table 5.1, GBP 1000 is equal to either USD 1651.50 or USD 1652. If a dealer is being asked to purchase GBP 1000 and to sell the equivalent amount of dollars, the trade will be done at 1.6515 since the dealer will only have to part with USD 1651.50 rather than USD 1652. However, if the dealer is being asked to sell sterling then the dealer would wish to obtain as many dollars as possible in exchange. The offer price would be used and the deal would be done at an exchange rate of 1.6520.

Similarly, in the second row of Table 5.1 the euro is the base currency. If the dealer is buying €1000 (the customer is selling) then they would wish to part with as few dollars as possible and the bid price would be used: USD 1382.50. If they were selling €1000 (the customer is buying) the offer price would be used and the dealer would receive USD 1383.

In the third row of Table 5.1 the dollar is the base currency. In this case the dealer will buy dollars and sell Swiss francs at 1.0535 (bid price). They would sell dollars and buy Swiss francs at 1.0540 (offer price).

For reference purposes, the midpoint price (mid price) is commonly used. This is the average of the bid and offer price, therefore: (bid + offer) divided by 2.

The size of the spread

The size of the spread is a function of market volatility, trading volume and competition. If the price is moving erratically, spreads will widen as traders become risk-averse. Greater market trading volume will tend to narrow spreads, and vice versa. The individual size of any transaction will also have a bearing: spreads will tend to widen with the size of the transaction as liquidity considerations come to bear. 'Liquidity' refers to the ability to trade without causing a significant movement in the price and with a minimum loss of value, within an expected amount of time. I shall be developing these points later, especially the importance of liquidity in trading and pricing.

While the opportunity for the market maker to make money increases with a wider spread, if the market maker quotes wider spreads relative to other dealers they risk not dealing at all. In principle, the aim of all foreign exchange trading operations is to deal as the market maker; in other words, dealing at your price. In the interbank market this is an essential condition of profitability as commissions are not charged on trades.

In the past there were opportunities to take advantage of price differentials between different markets, known as 'arbitrage'. Nowadays prices are transparent, seen on services such as Reuters and Bloomberg, and are quoted the same in all financial centres. Arbitrage in the old sense is no longer possible, although in recent years algorithmic trading models combined with super-fast computers have been able to replicate the arbitrage process for micro returns on a huge volume of transactions. I shall be talking about the growth of this practice – also known as high frequency trading – in chapter 6.

Direct and indirect quotations

Sometimes you will see reference to indirect and direct quotations. As in all dealings, it is essential to understand which is the base currency at the outset.

- An *indirect quote* is expressed as the number of foreign currency units per one domestic currency unit. Using the figures in Table 5.1, and from a European perspective, a euro is quoted indirectly and represents USD 1.3825. The pound against the dollar is invariably quoted on an indirect basis from a UK perspective since in Table 5.1 GBP 1 = USD 1.6515.

- A *direct quote* is expressed as the number of domestic currency units per one foreign currency unit. Using EUR/USD as an example, a European observer would obtain a direct quote by simply taking the reciprocal of 1.3825 (1/1.3825), which represents USD 1 = EUR 0.7233. This is a very useful tool for switching the quote base.

Most UK nationals would think in terms of GBP/EUR but the market convention is EUR/GBP. If EUR/GBP is 0.8800, GBP/EUR is simply the reciprocal of 0.8800 (1/0.8800), which equals 1.1364.

With the exceptions of the euro and the pound all exchange rates with the dollar are given as direct quotes, for example USD 1 = 1.0535 Swiss francs, or USD 1 = JPY 91.30. In the US, at least for domestic purposes, it is common for rates to be quoted as one foreign unit equalling so many dollars (therefore direct quotes from the American perspective).

Cross rates

The term 'cross rate' is normally used to refer to currency quotes which do not involve the US dollar, regardless of which country the quote is provided in. For instance, in London GBP/CHF and GBP/JPY are considered cross rates. The exchange rate between two currencies, both of which are not the official currencies of the country in which the exchange rate quote is given, are also considered cross rates. For example, CHF/JPY quoted in New York or London is a cross rate.

Thus, we can calculate the exchange rate for GBP/EUR, GBP/CHF and other crosses. Let's take an example and calculate GBP/CHF, assuming the exchange rates shown in Tables 5.2a and 5.2b are in place:

Table 5.2a – GBP/USD

Bid	Offer
GBP 1 = 1.6515	GBP 1 = 1.6520
Dealer's buy rate for pounds and sell rate for US dollars as market maker.	Dealer's selling rate for pounds and buying rate for US dollars as market maker.

Table 5.2b – USD/CHF

Bid	Offer
USD 1 = 1.0535	USD 1 = 1.0540
Dealer's buy rate for US dollars and sell rate for Swiss francs as market maker.	Dealer's sell rate for US dollars and buy rate for Swiss francs as market maker.

Therefore the rate at which a dealer will buy pounds and sell Swiss francs – the bid price for GBP/CHF – can be calculated by taking the buying rate for pounds (and the selling rate for dollars) and the selling rate for Swiss francs (and the buying rate for dollars).

To calculate GBP/CHF using the above rates:

GBP 1 = USD 1.6515 or USD 1 = GBP 1/1.6515 (reciprocal)

USD 1 = CHF 1.0535

Therefore (substituting in 1/1.6515 for USD 1) CHF 1.0535 = GBP 1/1.6515

CHF 1.0535 x 1.6515 = GBP 1

Therefore GBP 1 = CHF 1.7399 (rounded)

HOW DEALERS COVER THEIR EXPOSURE

To the customer the bank is the market maker. The bank who will attempt to cover the transaction in the market may not necessarily be so. A useful way to better understand this is to look at how a dealer might cover his exposure and to take a close look at cash flow movements. We are now beginning to look at positions, which are a key concept in trading.

Example – a customer sells GBP and buys CHF

Let's say a customer goes to their dealer (a bank) and sells GBP 1m and buys CHF at 1.7399 (the exact rate being CHF 1.739855).

In foreign exchange two currencies are always involved: one that is bought, the other that is sold. If a dealer buys a currency then they are said to be *long* or to have a *long position*. If a dealer has sold a currency then they are said to be *short* or to have a *short position*.

In this example, as the customer has sold sterling and bought Swiss francs, the dealer is long sterling and short Swiss francs. The bank position is:

Long sterling	Short Swiss francs
+ GBP 1,000,000	- CHF 1,739,855

Therefore, to reduce this position to zero, the dealer will have to sell GBP 1m and buy CHF.

In most cases, as in this example, cover would be obtained through the components of the cross, i.e., GBP/USD and USD/CHF. This would be the case for most sterling crosses, although one distinction is in the case of EUR/GBP, which is quoted in its own right in the market.

If we assume the rates are unchanged (a big assumption, made for illustrative purpose) when the bank balances up the position to zero, the dealer would look to deal with another bank in the market. They are no longer the market maker for the customer but are now the price taker and have to deal at another bank's price.

In this case the dealer will sell sterling and buy dollars at 1.6515, and sell dollars and buy Swiss francs at 1.0535 (as mentioned, the rates are unchanged from those given in the bid column of Tables 5.2a and 5.2b).

GBP 1,000,000 sold at a rate of 1.6515 = USD 1,651,500

USD 1,651,500 sold at a rate of 1.0535 = CHF 1,739,855

Referring back to the bank's position, which was + GBP 1,000,000 and - CHF 1,739,855, we can see that the bank has now a net position of zero. In this instance no profit or loss has been incurred.

However, if the market uses the dealer's prices the picture is rather different. In this case the bank will sell sterling and buy dollars at 1.6520 and sell dollars and buy Swiss francs at 1.0540 (these prices are taken from the offer columns of Tables 5.2a and 5.2b).

+ CHF 1,739,855 bought at 1.0540 = - USD 1,650,716

+ USD 1,650,072 bought at 1.6520 = - GBP 999,223

In this case a profit has been made of GBP 777 (GBP 1,000,000 - GBP 999,223). This may seem small but if this is multiplied by thousands of trades a day it becomes significant.

Example – a customer buys GBP and sells CHF

If the customer now wants to buy GBP 1m *against* CHF (they are selling CHF for GBP) the dealer will need to buy GBP from the market to sell to the customer. This is done at the market maker's selling rate for GBP against USD, which is 1.6520. In order to procure the USD the dealer will sell the CHF which was received from our customer at their rate of 1.0540.

To calculate the selling rate for GBP against CHF:

GBP 1 = USD 1.6520 or USD 1 = GBP 1/1.6520 (the reciprocal of 1.6520) = GBP 0.6053

USD 1 = CHF 1.0540

Therefore, CHF 1.0540 = GBP 1/1.6520

Therefore, 1.0540 x 1.6520 = GBP 1

Therefore, GBP 1 = 1.7412

As before, by covering with another bank's prices, no profit is made.

- Bank position -GBP 1,000,000, +CHF 1,741,200

- +GBP 1,000,000 bought at 1.6520 = -USD 1,652,000

- +USD 1,652,000 bought at 1.0540 = -CHF 1,741,208

There is a small CHF difference due to rounding.

Further example using cross rates

Table 5.3 – Cross rates for USD/JPY and USD/CHF

	Bid/Offer
USD/JPY	91.20/91.25
USD/CHF	1.0535/1.0540

The customer wishes to sell CHF 1m and buy JPY, so we need to deduce the buying rate for CHF.

The dealer will sell CHF against USD, that is they buy USD at the bank's selling price at 1.0540. They then buy JPY and sell USD, that is they sell USD at the bank's buying rate of 91.20.

Thus:

- USD 1 = CHF 1.0540

- USD 1 = JPY 91.20

- Therefore, CHF 1.0540 = JPY 91.20

- So, CHF 1 = 91.20/1.0540 = 86.53 = CHF buying rate

- Bank position + CHF 1,000,000, -JPY 86,530,000

To balance their position the bank must sell CHF 1m and buy JPY.

- Thus, CHF 1,000,000 sold at 1.0540 = +USD 948,767

- -USD 948,767 sold at 91.20 = +JPY 86,527,550

There is a small JPY difference due to rounding (-JPY 86,530,000 + JPY 86,527,550 = -2450).

Again, dealing at market prices will not yield any profit for the dealer.

Covering exposure and making a profit

To generate consistent profits the bank needs to deal off its own prices in volume. This, in practice, has always been the dealing proposition but has been aggressively pursued in recent years by a number of banks which now dominate the foreign exchange market.

This has coincided with the developments of dealing platforms designed to suck in ever larger foreign exchange volumes. The objective is to create a sufficient critical mass of client liquidity such that the clients automatically match off trades amongst themselves. This is now referred to as the *internalisation* of flows.

The ideal practice is not to be completely matched, even via customers, as returns would be too low, and importantly it would limit the ability to provide client liquidity at all times. The market maker will not cover every trade in full and is therefore creating a position. This is sometimes referred to as *warehousing trades*. This can improve their ability to meet their customer requirements and also allows the dealer to take advantage of market moves.

Of course the obvious way for a market maker to make a profit is to widen the spread or simply add a margin to the side requested. This is virtually impossible to achieve with large corporates, multinationals, funds and central banks. This is because there is such intense competition to obtain their business by the banks as they generate significant foreign exchange volume and provide directional information. For smaller companies and individuals this is possible in part because of relationship ties (accounts, investments, lending), but also because the size of transaction is usually quite small (a small transaction could be considered to be one under GBP 1m, EUR 1m or USD 1m).

The price that a market maker offers to customers will often differ from that seen on Reuters or Bloomberg screens, for example. These are subscription-based services which show wholesale or interbank indicative prices. These are quoted the same in all financial centres. These prices will generally be for a minimum and maximum size which is a function of market conditions.

Some internet sites will show similar prices for major currencies but these are sometimes slow to update and not especially reliable. Market makers will offer different prices because they are widening the spread to make a profit and also because small trades are not covered when they trade but are included in their overall positions.

Legging

A quote for EUR/GBP would be calculated by using quotes for GBP/USD and EUR/USD. When this is done, the GBP/USD and EUR/USD prices are referred to as 'legs'.

If the bank has been sold EUR/GBP it may wish to trade EUR/USD first and leave GBP/USD for later. For example, a customer sells EUR 5m versus GBP. The bank could sell EUR 5m vs. GBP immediately and the deal would be covered. Another option would be to leg. This means the bank could sell EUR 5m vs. USD first. This is illustrated in Table 5.4.

Table 5.4 – Bank position having bought GBP and sold EUR (EUR/GBP), then sold EUR and bought USD (EUR/USD)

Customer	+ EUR 5m	- GBP
Bank	- EUR 5m	+ USD

The bank's EUR position is now square, or zero, but the bank is short GBP and long USD. The decision process in legging could have been led by a desire to cover the most volatile currency pair or the view that GBP will depreciate in the short term (meaning that when GBP is bought back later it will be cheaper). In this particular case, EUR/USD is the most liquid currency pair.

To square this position the bank will buy GBP and sell USD.

There is an additional factor in that the bank may already be long GBP/USD from another trade or trades and in this scenario there would then be no requirement to go to the market. The final picture (from the bank's viewpoint) is shown in Table 5.5.

Table 5.5 – The final position of a legged trade from the bank's viewpoint

Customer	+ EUR 5m	- GBP
Bank	- EUR 5m	+USD
Bank	+ GBP	- USD

There are other considerations which lead to legging an order, especially a large one. For example, if a customer was selling GBP 400m vs. USD.

A trade of this size would move the market in most conditions and cable (GBP/USD) liquidity has a remarkable habit of drying up. For this reason this trade could not realistically be done in one go and would be broken up into small trades. If the market hears or senses that there is a large order there is the risk that the price could run lower. A solution for the bank is to trade in more liquid pairs, which also helps to disguise the underlying trade. In the case of the GBP 400m trade, the bank might trade in EUR/USD and EUR/GBP. The final picture (from the bank's viewpoint) is shown in Table 5.6.

Table 5.6 – The final position of another legged trade from the bank's viewpoint

Customer	+GBP	-USD
Bank	-EUR	+USD
Bank	+EUR	-GBP

ORDERS

In the equity markets an order is a request to make a trade. In the foreign exchange market an order is viewed as a request to make a trade when a price is reached, which would be referred to as a 'limit order' in the equity market. Orders are regularly placed in the market either to take a profit or to stop a loss. Orders can be made by all market participants, although a majority of stop loss orders are made by traders at financial institutions.

Orders are regularly left at technical pressure points (which I discuss in more detail in the technical analysis section of this book). At times these levels are considered so important by the market that orders become concentrated around these points. As a result, when these levels are broken, a sharp price reaction can ensue. Having a grasp of where such orders lie is essential when trading. It is not a failsafe guide to price direction (for instance, a very large order to sell could be absorbed by general market buying) but order knowledge provides another layer of information.

When leaving orders, especially for individuals, it is important to ascertain if the bank is taking a margin and what the size of the margin is. For instance, a take profit order at GBP/USD 1.60 with no margin would be executed at 1.60. If there was a margin of 25 pips this could be dealt with in two ways. If 1.60 was reached this would translate to 1.5975 for the customer. However, if the customer wished to receive 1.60 net the order would have to be set at 1.6025 in the market. This situation needs to be clearly explained by the dealer.

The ability of a bank to procure orders from its clients is important for internal liquidity, its ability to price other clients and manage its own dealing positions, and in turn generate a profit. In other words, the bank can match buyers and sellers at its prices rather than having to go to the market. For the major foreign exchange providers about 25% of turnover is now generated by the order book. Electronic trading platforms (e-commerce) incorporate sophisticated electronic order books. Some integrate client order flows with that of the dealing desk; others allow clients to match orders with other clients. In both these cases it can enable the client to deal within the market spread at the time.

I will now look at the main types of orders.

Take profit order

A take profit order is a contract with a bank to buy or sell an amount of currency at the rate specified, which would be a better rate than that currently available in the foreign exchange market for such a transaction.

For example, taking profit from a long position: in GBP/USD I buy GBP 1m at 1.60 and leave an order to sell GBP 1m at 1.65. If taking profit from a short position: in GBP/USD I sell GBP 1m at 1.60 and leave an order to buy at 1.55.

These orders can be executed on a manual or one-touch basis. The foreign exchange order will be filled manually by the bank's trading personnel if and when they determine, using reasonable efforts, that firm quotations are obtainable in the foreign exchange market for such a transaction at the order rate (taking account of any spread charged by the bank).

If the bank offers an electronic dealing platform the order will be filled automatically if and when the indicative rate shown (which may include any spread charged by the bank) reaches (i.e. one-touch basis) or exceeds the order rate specified in the order. A take profit order is placed on a *good till cancelled* or *good till a specified time* basis and may be withdrawn prior to execution but not while in the process of being executed.

Stop loss order

A stop loss order is a contract with a bank to buy or sell an amount of currency at the rate specified, which would be a worse rate than that currently available in the foreign exchange market for such a transaction. The importance of the stop loss order is that it will minimise losses if the trade has been taken in the wrong direction.

Taking the long position example above, I buy GBP 1m at 1.60 with a profit target at 1.6500. However, I do not want to incur losses below 1.57. I therefore will leave an order to sell GBP 1m at 1.57. Similarly, from the short position where I sold GBP 1m at 1.60, the stop loss order will be to buy GBP 1m at 1.63.

These orders can also be executed on a manual, one-touch or managed basis. A managed stop loss order will be executed when the indicative rate on the electronic platform exceeds the stop loss order rate by the amount of slippage. This is effectively the market bid-offer spread by reference to market conditions. The advantage of this method is that you know you have gone through the level, as opposed to the one-touch, which would close you out of the trade once the price level is hit but not necessarily penetrated. Setting up a managed order can increase your costs.

Banks leave themselves plenty of flexibility in execution and can revert to manual execution if they consider that a foreign exchange rate used to execute orders on a one-touch basis is unsupported due to the size of the order or through lack of liquidity or extreme volatility. A stop loss order is placed on a *good till cancelled* or *good till a specified time* basis and may be withdrawn prior to execution but not while in the process of being executed.

Stop loss orders are fraught with potential problems. The main issue is if the market or electronic trading system moves through the order rate without touching it. This is referred to as *gapping*. The next price could be some way off, increasing the loss on the trade. The bank is obliged to trade at the next available price and this can come as a shock if not previously explained. There is also the possibility that in times of market panic liquidity fails and dealing sizes shrink. It may not be possible to fill all of the order at the desired rate with the result that the balance has to be executed at a worse price. This is referred to as 'slippage'.

Stop loss orders will usually have the greatest market impact and on some occasions can signpost a major turn in direction. Unfortunately, forecasts do not always materialise. Their importance is to manage positions: to keep losses within defined limits, to take a profit and to take advantage of any upside while having some protection in place.

Call order

A call order is a monitoring service which enables the customer to receive notification from the bank if the rate reaches or exceeds the order rate specified by the customer. Notifications can be made by telephone but are increasingly relayed via email or SMS message. The bank will usually put a large disclaimer on this and it is effectively on a best efforts basis.

One Cancels Other (OCO) order

An OCO order is a combination of the same or different types of order, for example a combined take profit and stop loss. This can be for either identical or different currency pairs, amounts and value dates. When the first of either order is filled the other order is cancelled.

A common application of an OCO is when a trader has a profit target but also wants to protect the downside. An OCO order is placed on *good until cancelled* or *good until a specified time* basis and applies to the component orders in an OCO order.

An OCO order may be withdrawn at any time unless the bank has executed or is in the process of doing so.

The component orders in an OCO order can be set to have different blackout periods, during which the relevant order will not be filled but may be cancelled if the other order is filled. A blackout period is a useful feature around price sensitive data releases or important foreign exchange fixing times when volatility can increase dramatically for a short period of time but where the underlying trend remains intact.

If Done Do Other (IDO) order

An IDO order is a combination of the same or different types of order, for example take profit and stop loss. This can be for either identical or different currency pairs, amounts and value dates.

The execution of the second order is conditional upon the first order being filled. An IDO order is usually placed on a *good until cancelled* or *good until a specified time* basis. An IDO order may be withdrawn at anytime unless the bank has executed or is in the process of doing so. The component orders in an IDO order can be set to have different blackout periods during which the relevant order will not be filled but may be cancelled if the other order is filled.

HOW TO CALCULATE TRADING PROFITS AND LOSSES

Calculating profits and losses is very important during a trade. It is very useful to have a shorthand method to know how much a certain movement impacts on the profit and loss. For instance, how would a 20 pip move in a long position of GBP 4.5m in GBP/USD affect the trade? In the example below I shall take a move from 1.4040 to 1.4020.

Example – a 20 pip move in a GBP 4.5m GBP/USD trade

To work out the effect of a 20 pip move from 1.4040 to 1.4020 in a GBP/USD trade you would multiply the position size by the old and new price, and then subtract the old price from the new. It is important to note that if one multiplies the points difference by the base currency the profit or loss will be shown in the alternative currency.

For example:

GBP 4.5m x 1.4040 = USD 6,318,000

GBP 4.5m x 1.4020 = USD 6,309,000

USD 6,309,000 - USD 6,318,000 = USD -9,000

This represents a loss of USD 9,000.

A shorthand method is:

GBP 4.5m x 0.0020 = USD 9,000

In the above example you may wish to take the loss in sterling. You would then sell USD 6,318,000 for GBP at 1.4020 = GBP 4,506,419.40, which is a loss of GBP 6,419.40.

Alternatively, the quick way to calculate this is:

GBP 4.5m x 0.0020 = USD 9,000

USD 9,000/1.4020 = GBP 6,419.40

Using a CHF/JPY cross the same process applies. I have bought CHF 5m and there has been a move from 81.20 to 81.00.

CHF 5m x 81.20 = JPY 406,000,000

CHF 5m x 81.00 = JPY 405,000,000

JPY 405,000,000 – JPY 406,000,000 = -JPY 1,000,000

This represents a loss of JPY 1,000,000

A shorthand method is:

CHF 5m x 0.20 = JPY 1,000,000.

To express the loss in CHF:

JPY 1m/81.00 = CHF 12,345.68

RECORDING A TRADE

Every trade must be recorded in the bank's books, confirmed to the customer and processed so that payment can be made on the agreed date. This process is now largely computerised with the following information being input by the trader:

- names of the customer or counterparty
- date of the transaction – the contract date
- value (or settlement) date of the transaction – in the case of a spot trade and a forward outright, in a swap there would be the near date (usually spot) and the far date
- currencies and amounts purchased and sold
- exchange rate at which the transaction has been executed; one rate will apply for a spot or forward trade but there will be two rates in a swap
- settlement instructions: where the funds sold are to be paid and how the funds bought are to be received
- source of trade: telephone, generated or broker
- name of dealer.

On completion of this input the bank's position is automatically updated. This is monitored by the dealers and the chief dealer, and positions are also supervised by an internal risk department.

The trade is then passed to the operations or back office department. They will:

- make the necessary account entries
- ensure SWIFT messages, etc., to make sure the payments are correct
- arrange for a confirmation contract note to be sent to the customer; in some organisations, where there is a forward contract, a duplicate is sent as a reminder nearer to the value date
- ensure that foreign nostro accounts have sufficient funds through daily projection of movements through these accounts
- produce accurate position records, both spot and forwards, for dealers and management, to ensure that the dealing department is adhering to management guidelines
- produce profit and loss figures, both spot and forward.

RULES WHEN MAKING FOREIGN EXCHANGE TRANSACTIONS

Buying and selling currency, at face value, would seem very straightforward but mistakes do occur. I have noted some simple guidelines here:

- Specify very clearly who is dealing (the full customer name, legal entity), the amount, the currency pair involved and the value (settlement) date.

- Keep the process simple. You should say, "I sell GBP 1m and buy CHF for spot value." Do not say "I want 1 million pounds worth" of CHF. That always gets people scratching their heads.

- Prices are not door numbers, they move. On receipt of a quote respond quickly. There is no holding period for a price: the market maker can change the price at any time by saying "change". Traders do not take kindly to being messed around. In certain circumstances the dealer can say "your risk", which means the price is subject to an automatic refresh if the customer wishes to deal.

- Amongst professional traders there is the practice of not quoting the full price but simply the last two decimals of the currency in question. This is based on the premise they know perfectly well what figures come in front. In volatile markets I suggest it is always best to get the full price.

- For very large transactions the customer should state whether or not they are asking for a price on their *full amount*. If the customer is doing the same transaction elsewhere they can move the price against you.

- Always confirm the trade details before hanging up. The time is well spent and does not make you look an amateur. There is nothing worse than having to go and listen to the tape recordings, hoping you are right.

- In most dealings between banks, or banks with corporates or individuals, some form of dealing limit will need to be pre-arranged. This is especially the case for transactions that settle beyond spot. It is very important that these are checked prior to dealing to ensure that agreements or limits are not breached. It is also important because opportunities may be missed if one cannot trade.

6.

TYPES OF FOREIGN EXCHANGE TRANSACTIONS

In this section we will look at the following foreign exchange transactions:

1. Spot

2. Forward

3. Broken date

4. Non-deliverable forward (NDF)

5. Swap

6. Forward/forward

7. Algorithmic trading

8. Options

1. SPOT

A spot transaction is the exchange of two currencies at an agreed rate for cash delivery (settlement). This means that transactions entered will be settled between the two contracting parties two business days later (except for transactions involving the Canadian dollar, which is settled one business day later) and is referred to as funds.

For example, a spot deal contracted on Monday will be settled on Wednesday and a spot deal contracted on Wednesday will be settled on Friday. A spot deal contracted on Thursday will be settled on Monday since all the major centres (London, New York, Frankfurt, Zurich, Tokyo) are closed at the weekend.

If a US dollar/Swiss franc (USD/CHF) spot trade has been made on the Thursday and the following Monday is a US holiday the transaction will not be settled (funds exchanged) until the Tuesday. However, even if a pound/Swiss franc (GBP/CHF) trade was made on the same Thursday the spot date would normally be quoted the Tuesday despite the centres being open. Market practice is not to trade on a US holiday, whatever the cross.

The two-day period between contract date and settlement date has its roots in arranging the administration and accounting for payments to be made.

While advances in technology have considerably improved this administration, one still cannot avoid trading for different time zones, for instance, dealing in London involving the sale of pounds for New Zealand dollars. The exchange date, or settlement date, is often referred to in the market as the 'value date'.

The two parties involved have entered into a foreign exchange contract. They both have an obligation to deliver the currency on the agreed day. There is no option involved. Neither is there any physical movement of funds – the transaction is simply the process of debiting or crediting another account.

All foreign exchange transactions are calculated relative to spot. There are a number of currencies that will allow trading against one other for same-day settlement (subject to cut-off times during the day). These are US dollar, euro, pound and Canadian dollar. Any transaction for settlement today or tomorrow, or longer than spot, will normally require an adjustment to the spot quotation unless the time being used is normal market practice. I shall be explaining this calculation later as a failure to understand can lead to incorrect quotes and potential losses.

When spot dates can be confusing

Here are some examples of how spot dates can become confusing, especially for dealers. Christmas, or any occasion when the markets are closed for a number of days in a short period, is a bad time for this.

Example 1

Let's say today is Tuesday 22 December 2009.

There is a Japanese holiday on Wednesday 23 December, a Swedish holiday on Thursday 24 December, a UK and market holiday on Friday 25 December, then on the weekend 26/27 December the market is closed, and then there is another UK holiday on 28 December.

This series of market holidays would result in the settlement dates shown in Table 6.1 for different currency pairs.

Table 6.1 – Effect of market holidays on settlement dates for currency pairs

Currency pair	Spot settlement date
GBP/USD	24/12/09
EUR/USD	24/12/09
USD/JPY	28/12/09
USD/SEK	28/12/09
GBP/JPY	29/12/09

You can see that GBP/USD and EUR/USD are straightforward, the settlement date remains at two business days. The USD/JPY and USD/SEK transactions are pushed to 28 December because both have holidays on 23 December. The UK holiday on 28 December has no impact on these transactions as neither currency will be settled in London. The GBP/JPY transaction (and all sterling crosses) are affected by the London holiday on 28 December as no sterling settlement is possible. The next working day for both is 29/12.

Example 2

Let's say that today is Wednesday 23 December 2009 (the holidays are the same as in Example 1).

This series of market holidays would result in the settlement dates shown in Table 6.2 for different currency pairs.

Table 6.2 – Effect of market holidays on settlement dates for different currency pairs

Currency pair	Spot settlement date
GBP/USD	29/12/09
EUR/USD	28/12/09
USD/JPY	28/1/209
USD/SEK	29/12/09
GBP/JPY	29/12/09
EUR/SEK	29/12/09

Sterling settlement has to be on 29 December because of the holiday on 28 December. EUR/USD is settled on 28 December because of Christmas Day and USD/JPY keeps the same settlement date. The Swedish holiday on 24 December now means spot will be 29/12, following the two business days rule.

Example 3

Let's say today is 24 December 2009 (the market holidays are the same as in Example 1).

This series of market holidays would result in the settlement dates shown in Table 6.3 for different currency pairs.

Table 6.3 – Effect of market holidays on settlement dates for different currency pairs

Currency pair	Spot settlement date
GBP/USD	30/12/09
EUR/USD	29/12/09
USD/JPY	28/12/09
USD/SEK	29/12/09
GBP/JPY	30/12/09
EUR/SEK	29/12/09

Sterling spot will settle on 30 December due to the holiday on 28 December, following the two business days rule. The same rule applies to EUR and SEK and as they do not have a holiday on the 28 December the spot is a day earlier on the 29 December. You will note that throughout these examples USD/JPY spot date has remained the same at 28/12. Market convention dictates this even though 25/12 is a universal holiday. This is a peculiarity of US holidays.

It is little surprise that spot dates can create a fair bit of confusion but it is very important to understand if errors in pricing are not to occur.

Examples of customer transactions

Example 1

ABC Plc need to make a payment of USD 5,000,000 value spot. GBP/USD is 1.6515-20 and today is 10 March.

ABC's Assistant Treasurer calls their bank's foreign exchange sales desk and asks for a quote on GBP/USD in USD 5,000,000 for value spot.

John from ABC – "Morning. This is John from ABC Plc. I would like a price in cable (GBP/USD) in USD 5,000,000 for spot value."

The dealer bank sales desk responds – "15-20."

John from ABC would then confirm – "At 15 ABC Plc buys USD 5,000,000."

The dealer bank sales desk would say – "To confirm, you bought USD 5,000,000 and sold GBP at 1.6515 value 12 March."

You will note the bank only quoted the last two numbers of the price. These are referred to as pips in the market. In practice, if a professional dealer is speaking to another professional dealer the quotation would rarely be 1.6515-1.6520. It is assumed that the other party was aware of the first part of the price. It is advisable, however, not to try and be too clever and if in any doubt ask and give the full price.

Note also that the value date is two business days on from the trade date. By quoting buying and selling rates a bank is committing itself to either buy or sell certain amounts at these prices. There are no written rules about the size of these amounts but they will vary according to the currency pair and market conditions. In this context market liquidity is important.

Example 2

ABC Plc needs to sell USD 5,000,000 and buy CHF value spot. USD/CHF is 1.0535-40 and today is 10 March.

ABC's Assistant Treasurer calls his bank and asks for a quote on USD/CHF in USD 5,000,000 for value spot.

John from ABC – "Hi, John here from ABC. I need to sell USD 5,000,000 and buy CHF value spot."

The dealer bank sales desk would respond with a price – "John you can sell the USD at 1.0535 value spot."

John from ABC – "Done." And would confirm the deal – "ABC Plc sell USD 5,000,000 and buy CHF at 1.0535 value 12 March."

The dealer bank sales desk would also confirm the deal – "Thanks John, to confirm you sold USD 5,000,000 and bought CHF at 1.0535 value 12 March."

In the first example ABC did not disclose its intention, or side, and requested a two-way price. The reason for this practice is simply the view that you will get a better price if you do not tell the bank which way you are trading. This is not always the case as in difficult trading conditions the bank may well widen the price.

In our example ABC was only asking one bank but they may well have lined up two or three to compare prices. Although there is an increasing use of electronic dealing platforms, direct dealing – over the phone, as in these examples – is still very prevalent, accounting for about 40% of transactions. Large transactions are still traded on a direct basis.

2. FORWARD OUTRIGHT

A foreign exchange *forward* is an exchange of two currencies at a predetermined rate for any date other than spot delivery. To avoid confusion when talking about forward business, dealers use the term *outright* when it is a single forward transaction as against a forward swap transaction.

The forward outright price is calculated in relation to the number of forward points (also referred to as swap points) added to or subtracted from the current spot rate. The forward points which are used to calculate an outright forward are themselves calculated from the interest rate differential between the two currencies. Therefore, forward points are only a reflection of the rate differentials between two currencies traded in money markets. Moreover, the forward points have nothing to do with exchange rate forecasts and make no direct statement of one currency strengthening or weakening against the other except in a theoretical sense (discussed further in chapter 4 'Theory of Foreign Exchange'). I will explain how to calculate and interpret forward points in this section.

A forward outright transaction attracts spot risk, which means that if the spot price moves the parties in the transaction are exposed to a potential loss or a potential profit.

Most forward/swap contracts are quoted for the following fixed periods:

- one month
- two months
- three months
- six months
- one year.

These periods are taken from the spot date, e.g., spot 1m (one month), spot 3m (three months). Other forward dates are possible and these are called broken date contracts (see 'Broken date contracts' on p.102). Also, for certain currencies start dates can be before spot. The vast majority of forward contracts are under six months but it is possible to obtain prices in excess of five years.

Forwards under one year would have broadly similar transactions cost to spot transactions and can be considered a cheap method to hedge future exposures. Maturities in excess of one year will start to become more expensive reflecting the increased risk. There may even be fees charged by the bank for providing the facility.

Forward outright quote – example 1

Forward outright exchange rates are those rates quoted today at which currency can be purchased or sold for delivery at some agreed date in the future. With a forward outright quote there is a buying and selling rate, and there is nearly always a spread between the buying and selling rate.

In this example AAA Plc is buying a gas turbine from the USA for USD 5m and payment for turbine is due on 7 October. Today is 3 April and the current GBP/USD prices are:

- Bid = 1.4365

- Offer = 1.4370

AAA decides to buy USD 5m and sell GBP on a six-month forward contract. The exchange of currencies will be on 7 October. The forward bid rate of 1.4220 is arrived at by applying the forward points to today's spot bid rate of 1.4365.

The summary details of the transaction are shown in Table 6.4. Note in particular the forward points that are applied to achieve the forward outright quote in both the bid and offer columns.

Table 6.4 – GBP/USD forward outright quote

	Bid	Offer
GBP/USD spot	1.4365	1.4370
Forward points	-0.0145	-0.0144
Forward outright six months GBP/USD	1.4220	1.4226
Customer view	Sell GBP (buy USD)	Buy GBP (sell USD)

This is how the conversation may have gone:

AAA's Assistant Treasurer calls his bank and asks for a quote to buy USD 5m six months forward.

John from AAA – "Hi, John here from AAA. I need to buy USD 5m vs. GBP six months forward. What is the outright price?"

Dealer bank sales – "John, you can buy the USD at 1.4220 value 7 October."

John from AAA – "Done, AAA buys USD 5m vs. GBP at 1.4220 value 7 October."

Dealer bank sales – "Thanks John. To confirm you bought USD 5m and sold GBP at 1.4220 value 7 October."

Therefore, AAA buys USD 5m and sells GBP 3,516,174.40 forward at 1.4220 on a six-month forward contract (5m/1.4220 = 3,516,174.40).

The advantage of this transaction from the point of view of AAA is that they have agreed to pay GBP 3,516,174.40 for the USD 5m on 7 October. If they had not entered the forward contract and sterling had depreciated against the dollar from April to October, the turbine would have cost them more than GBP 3,516,174.40.

Forward outright quote – example 2

Now let's assume ABC Plc needs to sell USD 5m and buy CHF in three months' time. Spot USD/CHF is 1.0535-40 and today is 10 March.

ABC's Assistant Treasurer calls his bank and asks for a quote on USD/CHF in USD 5m for value in three months.

John from ABC – "Hi, John here from ABC. I need to sell USD 5m and buy CHF value in three months. Can I have a price please?"

Dealer bank sales – "John can we confirm the date please? If you are looking at spot/three months (standard period convention) the date will be 12 June."

John from ABC – "That date is agreed. What are the points?"

Dealer bank sales – "Spot/three months points are -25."

John from ABC – "OK, quote me the spot and we shall deal with the adjustment afterwards."

Dealer bank sales – "35."

John from ABC – "Done. ABC Plc sells USD 5m and buys CHF at 1.0510 value 12 June."

Dealer bank sales – "Thanks John. To confirm you sold USD 5m and bought CHF at 1.0510 value 12 June."

It is always a good idea to confirm the date because forwards are normally quoted from the spot date. It is also worth checking the date is a good day, i.e., not a market holiday or weekend.

As a general rule forward points will not move much during a quote while the spot price can move significantly. There is also the practical consideration of trying to quote a forward outright price when prices are moving. This example is for a short period and the forward points are not a major consideration. However, with forward contracts over a longer period, especially over a year, the forward points can be an important factor.

In the example above ABC was concerned about the spot. In other circumstances ABC might have gone to a number of banks to get their forward prices as a means of comparison.

How to calculate and interpret forward/swap points

In calculating the forward points a formula is used which accounts for the interest rate differential in the money markets between the two currencies (not the official bank interest rates), plus the period of time the forward is outstanding. These factors are used in relation to the current spot rate.

It is important to note that interest rate day counts can be different. The day count determines how interest accrues over time. For sterling, interest is calculated by taking the actual number of days over 365 days (actual/365). In a Leap Year this will be actual/366 (actual/actual). For US dollars interest is calculated with actual/360, as it is for the euro, yen and Swiss franc.

Forward points = spot x (1 + (OCR rate x (n/360))/(1+(BCR rate x (n/360)) - spot

OCR = Other currency interest rate

BCR = Base currency interest rate

Simple interest calculation = (1 + rate of interest)

n = number of days/period of time the forward is outstanding

Forward points must be added to or subtracted from the spot rate to find the forward rate. The rule is that if the forward points are ascending from left to right (LO to HI – discounts) you add them to the spot rate to find the forward rate. If forward points are descending (HI to LO – premiums) then you subtract the points from the spot rate to find the forward rate.

An easy way to determine which currency has the higher interest rates is to refer to the forward quote, which always starts with the base currency. For GBP/USD, sterling is the base currency. If the forward points are quoted 145/144, put these numbers under GBP/USD. The higher figure 145 is now under GBP and the lower figure 144 is now under USD. This indicates that sterling has the higher interest rate and USD interest rates are lower than sterling interest rates. In this situation the points are going from HI to LO (145 is higher than 144) and so they should be subtracted from the spot rate to find the forward rate.

Example 1 – GBP/USD forward points

GBP/USD has forward points 145-144.

Table 6.5 – Example of GBP/USD forward points

Sterling	Dollar
Forward points 145	Forward points 144
HI	LO
High interest rate currency	Low interest rate currency
Currency at discount	Currency at premium
Sterling is at a discount to the dollar	Dollar is at a premium to sterling

In this situation the points are HI to LO so you would subtract the points from the spot rate to find the forward rate.

Example 2 – USD/NOK forward points

The USD/NOK cross has forward points 320-350.

Table 6.6 – Example of USD/NOK forward points

Dollar	Norwegian krona
Forward points 320	Forward points 350
LO	HI
Low interest rate currency	High interest rate currency
Currency at premium	Currency at discount
Dollar is at a premium to the Norwegian krona	Norwegian krona is at a discount to the dollar

In this situation the points are LO to HI so you would add them to the spot rate to find the forward rate.

It is worth emphasising that the forward points (normally) represent interest rate differentials between the two currencies. As interest rates move, so do the forward points. As a general rule forward points are less volatile than the spot price but during the financial crisis of 2008-09 there was considerable movement as interest rates moved dramatically.

Occasionally, one will see forward points that have a negative number for one side of the quote and a positive number for the other side (e.g., -5, +20). The rules for adding or subtracting still hold. This pricing occurs when the interest rates of the two currencies are so close that the offer side of one crosses the bid side of the other, e.g., sterling interest rate 1.45%/1.38%; dollar interest rate 1.5%/1.43%.

Alternative method of creating a forward contract

It is possible to replicate a forward outright transaction through borrowing and lending.

Let's say a customer wants to buy USD 5m against GBP, six-month forward. The trade details are shown in Table 6.7 and the breakdown of the trade is shown in Table 6.8.

Table 6.7 – Trade details for an alternative method of forward

Trade date	3 April
GBP/USD spot	1.4365
USD six-month interest rate	2.25% (lend)
GBP six-month interest rate	4.32% (borrow)
Maturity	185 days

Table 6.8 – Breakdown of the alternative forward trade

USD	GBP
5,000,000	3,480,682.21
185 days @ 2.25%	185 days @ 4.32%
Interest = USD 57,812.50	Interest = GBP 76,212.64
USD = 5,057,812.50	GBP = 3,556,894.85

Customer borrows GBP and sells for USD 5m to lock in the current spot rate. This USD 5m is then placed on deposit for six months.

The forward rate is calculated as follows (dividing the dollar amount with interest by the pound amount with interest):

USD 5,057,812.50/GBP 3,556,894.85 = 1.42197

The forward points are:

1.4365 - 1.42197 = 0.01453

To calculate via the formula:

Forward points = ((spot x (1 + USD rate x (n/360)))/(1 + (GBP rate x (n/365)))) - spot

= ((1.4365 x (1 + 0.0225 x 185/360)))/((1 + (0.432 x (185/365)))) - 1.4365

= 0.01453

Value date option forwards

At times, there might be a desire to hedge foreign exchange exposure with a forward contract but there is uncertainty as to when funds are due or to be received. Typical examples include an individual buying a property abroad, a film company making payments over the period of a production, or a company importing or exporting where payment may be based on when the ship docks or the day bills of lading are presented.

To overcome this problem the customer can enter into a value date option, or window, contract with a bank. As is the case with a normal forward, a rate is agreed for future delivery but with the added benefit of being able to take up the contract in whole or parts between two agreed rates in the future. It is important to note that, despite the name, there is no option (in the sense of a derivative financial product) involved in this contract. The use of *option* in the name relates purely to timing – there is an obligation to settle within the contract dates agreed.

In return for this extra flexibility the bank would normally make the price of the contract more expensive than a forward for a specific value date.

Example of a value date option forward

An importer wishes to buy a USD 1m option for a two- to three-month window and sell pounds. The prices shown in Table 6.9 apply in the market.

Table 6.9 – The prices for the value date option

Spot GBP/USD	1.6171/1.6177
Swap (forward) points two months	68/67
Swap (forward) points three months	104/103

The swap points are premiums and these points are subtracted from the spot to arrive at the forward outright price. It is therefore more expensive to buy dollars forward because dollars are at a premium to sterling. The option to buy dollars can be taken up by the customer up to the end of three months, so the bank would quote 1.6067 (1.6171 - 0.0104). This is the best price which the bank can offer if they wish to fully cover their exposure, which could last until the end of the third month.

If the customer were an exporter and was receiving USD 1m instead, they would be looking to sell USD 1m. Using the rates above the bank would quote for a two- to three-month option 1.6110 (1.6177 - 0.0067). Again this is the best rate the bank can offer on the assumption that the customer sells at the earliest date.

The risk for the bank is interest rate exposure as the actual settlement date is as yet unknown. The bank has to decide how to cover its exposure. For the bank, covering the forward to the earliest date is often the most sensible. The majority of trades tend to be taken up relatively quickly as clients tend to view the product as an insurance policy, adding on days to allow for minor delays to their plans. As necessary, short-dated swaps are used to bridge the gap between the date that is covered to by the bank and the actual settlement date.

If the bank priced this contract for the customer to sell dollars at a three-month rate the customer would get 1.6074 (1.6177 - 0.0103), which for the customer is 36 points better than if they sold at the earliest date (1.6110). However, the bank has to price at the two-month rate if it does not want to incur a potential loss on the deal.

The bank is quoting the worst price to the customer simply because it does not know when the customer will take up the contract.

If the customer settles on any date other than the first possible (two months) then clearly the original price was not the best which could have been achieved.

Dealing to a precise date therefore has a price advantage, in this case potentially 36 points. For a small company or individuals dealing in relatively small amounts the value date option method has attractions. It is simple and flexible. Those dealing in large amounts would deal for a precise date. If the funds were not available at the contract date then a foreign exchange swap would be used to roll the contract forward. This process will be explained in the next section.

3. BROKEN DATE CONTRACTS

As mentioned above, most foreign exchange contracts are quoted for fixed periods of months or years. A broken date is a forward transaction, the maturity of which is for a date other than a natural month end, e.g., 45 days (between one month and two months). In order to price a broken dated contract it is necessary to interpolate between the two dates. For simplicity, I will use middle prices. The calculation method used is shown in Table 6.10.

Table 6.10 – Calculating forward points for broken date contracts

One-month forward swap points 32	One month = 31 days
Two-months forward swap points 64	Two months = 63 days
Swap day gap	63 days - 31 days = 32 days
Swap price gap	64 points - 32 points = 32 points
One month against 45 day broken date	45 days - 31 days = 14 days
Two months against 45 day broken date	63 days - 45 days = 18 days
The points are worth per day 1 month vs. 2 months	32 points/32 days = 1
Swap price gap	14 days x 1 point per day = 14 or 18 days x 1 point per day = 18
45 day price calculated from the one month swap	32 + 14 = 46 points
45 day price calculated from the two month swap	64 - 18 = 46 points

While the banks prefer to quote straight dates, companies and individuals rarely have this luxury. It is important to understand how broken dated points are calculated to avoid mis-pricing. I have selected a simple example when the days have equal value. This is not always the case and at certain periods when huge funding and loan fixes occur – such as month, quarter and year end, and Christmas – there can be large distortions.

Short dates

Although most foreign exchange transactions are executed for a value date two days ahead (spot) or for longer (forward) it is possible for some currencies (essentially confined to GBP, EUR and CAD) to deal for the same day or the next day. The terminology for the short time periods is shown in Table 6.11.

Table 6.11 – Terminology for short foreign exchange contract periods

Value same day	Overnight (O/N)
Value tomorrow	Tom next (T/N)
Value day after spot (three days)	Spot next (S/N)

The rates quoted for value dates occurring before spot are treated in a different way from those occurring after spot. Before spot, funds are either being paid away early or received early. This swap adjustment process is to compensate for any interest rate gain or loss that arises from this.

If the value date is before spot the points should be switched and the normal rule is observed: if points go LO to HI, they should be added to spot; if points go HI to LO, they should be subtracted from spot.

If value same day is quoted the overnight and tomorrow next prices will be added together and then switched. The S/N price is after spot and the normal rule is followed.

Table 6.12 shows how points are applied to short-dated transactions.

Example – GBP/USD

Table 6.12 – Applying points to spot for short foreign exchange contract periods

Spot	1.6171-1.6177
O/N points	2-1
Outright value today	The 2-1 points are added to the 2-1 points for T/N and then swapped to give points of 2-4. These points are then added to the spot as they now read LO to HI.
1.6173 (1.6171 + 0.0002) - 1.6181 (1.6177 + 0.0004)	
T/N points	2-1
Outright value tomorrow	The 2-1 points are swapped to 1-2 and then added to the spot as they now read LO to HI.
1.6172 (1.6171 + 0.0001) - 1.6179 (1.6177 + 0.0002)	
S/N points	3-2
Outright value three days	The S/N date is after spot and so the points are not swapped. As 3-2 reads HI to LO the points are subtracted from spot.
1.6168 (1.6171 - 0.0003) - 1.6175 (1.6177 - 0.0002)	

The daily cut-off times to deal for same day settlement will vary from bank to bank. In my current post it is 1.30 pm for EUR and 3.30 pm for GBP/USD and CAD, but this will not necessarily always be the case. For some currencies, such as JPY and Scandinavian currencies, the next day will be the earliest value date for a transaction. The issue is whether the entries can be made and the funds used by the receiving bank. This will determine what value date can be given.

Dealing end/end

When a settlement date falls on month end, forward settlement for standard forward dates follows the end/end convention. As forward prices are generated from the money markets this practice is applied in both the money and foreign exchange markets. This as best illustrated through examples, initially showing how we deal with straight dates at month end.

Example 1

On 29 January forward contracts are dealt in the one-month, three-month and six-month (29 January is a normal trading day).

- If 29 February (this is a leap year) falls on a Sunday the forward date for the one-month contract will be 27 February.
- If 30 April falls on a Saturday the forward date for the three-month contract will be 29 April.
- If 31 July falls on a bank holiday the forward date for the six-month contract will be 30 July.
- The key feature of the forward dates is that they are not taken over into a new month.

Example 2

If 31 January falls on a Sunday then the last working day in the month will be 29 January. If, as in the previous example, contracts are dealt in the one-month, three-month and six-month these will be executed on 27 January.

As before:

- If 29 February (this is a leap year) falls on a Sunday the forward date for the one-month contract will be 27 February.
- If 30 April falls on a Saturday the forward date for the three-month contract will be 29 April.
- If 31 July falls on a bank holiday the forward date for the six-month contract will be 30 July.

In the last case you may have expected the six-month date to be 29 July. The date has been stretched to the end of the month (last working day). Similarly, if 30 April falls on a Friday this would have been the forward date.

To illustrate further, if this was not a leap year there would be 28 days in February. If 28 February fell on a Sunday the last working day of the month is 26 February and forward contracts would be dealt on 24 February. In this case the forward dates would be the same as those shown above in the examples, not the 26th of each month. Thus the contracts have been dealt from month-end to month-end, i.e., end/end.

The day count in these contracts is different from what you would intuitively expect and will impact on the price.

4. NON-DELIVERABLE FORWARD (NDF)

A non-deliverable forward (NDF) is a forward transaction used to hedge non-convertible currencies. These currencies include:

- Indian rupee

- Taiwan dollar

- Korean won

- Chinese renminbi

- Philippine peso

- Indonesian rupee

- Malaysian ringgit

- Argentine peso

- Chilean peso

- Columbian peso

- Peruvian nuevo sol

- Russian rouble.

These contracts were developed for emerging markets where capital controls and restrictions on forward trading were in operation. The primary use of NDFs has been speculative. The Chinese renminbi has, in this context, been the primary traded currency as traders have speculated over renminbi revaluation.

NDF is a forward outright contract in which two counterparties settle the difference between the contracted NDF rate (forward rate) and the prevailing spot price on an agreed notional amount of the non-convertible currency. These special NDF contracts must meet the provisions of the internationally recognised International Swaps and Derivatives Association (ISDA).

As with a forward transaction, the NDF rate corresponds to the spot rate adjusted for the interest rate differential between the two currencies; however, unlike a normal forward outright, there is never an exchange of principal.

If you believe the non-deliverable currency will weaken against the settlement currency (i.e., you are effectively receiving the non-deliverable currency in the future) you will enter into an NDF where you elect to sell the non-deliverable currency and purchase the settlement currency on the maturity date.

Alternatively, if you believe the non-deliverable currency will strengthen against the settlement currency (i.e., you are effectively paying the non-deliverable currency in the future) you will enter into an NDF where you elect to purchase the non-deliverable currency and sell the settlement currency on the maturity date.

The fixing date is the day and time when the comparison between the NDF rate and the current spot rate is made and is normally two business days before the settlement date. The settlement date is the day when the difference is paid or received.

NDFs are normally quoted with the US dollar as the reference currency but other currencies such as euro and Swiss francs are also possible; the settlement amount is also in dollars. No payment or account movement takes place in the non-convertible currency.

When a NDF is agreed the parties must also agree on a way to determine the reference rate at the fixing date (maturity). The spot rate on the fixing date is usually provided by the central bank but can be an average rate published by several banks. For example, the official spot fixing rate for US dollar/Chinese renminbi is reported by The State Administration of Foreign Exchange of the People's Republic of China, Beijing, which appears on Reuters at approximately 5 pm, Beijing time, on that rate calculation date.

NDF tenors usually follow the IMM (International Monetary Market) dates, although other dates will be quoted on request. IMM dates are the third Wednesday of March, June, September and December.

The NDF can be terminated at any time up to and including the fixing date. At any time up to the fixing date the maturity date can be brought forward.

Example

ABC Company imports goods from China. ABC is billed in Chinese Renmindi (CNY) but has to pay in USD. The latest invoice is to pay the USD equivalent of CNY 10m in six months' time. Assume the current USD/CNY exchange rate for spot value is 6.46.

If ABC did nothing, the amount of USD that ABC will be obliged to pay in six months' time will depend on the USD/CNY foreign exchange rates at that time.

For example, if the USD/CNY foreign exchange rate rises to 6.76, the USD amount required will be:

USD 1,479,289.94 (CNY 10,000,000/6.76)

Alternatively, if the USD/CNY market foreign exchange rate falls to 6.16, the USD amount required will be:

USD 1,623,376.62 (CNY 10,000,000/6.16)

If ABC wishes to protect against the USD depreciating against the CNY, ABC will enter into a USD/CNY NDF with a notional amount of CNY 10m and set a contract rate for six months' time. The bank gives ABC a rate of 6.5, and the fixing methodology is agreed.

Possible outcomes

1. If the fixing rate on the fixing date is less favourable to ABC than the contract rate, the bank will pay ABC the cash settlement in USD on the maturity date.

So, say the fixing rate for USD/CNY is 6.16, the fixing settlement amount will be:

USD 1,623,376.62 (CNY 10,000,000/6.16)

While the contract settlement amount will be:

USD 1,538,461.54 (CNY 10,000,000/6.50)

The difference of USD 84,915.08 will be paid by the bank to ABC on the maturity date.

The cash settlement amount will compensate ABC for the higher USD amount that ABC will need to pay for the goods. To purchase the goods ABC would have to pay USD 1,623,376.62. With the benefit of the USD cash settlement amount ABC receives under the NDF (USD 84,915.08) ABC's total outlay will be reduced to USD 1,538,461.54, which is equivalent to a USD/CNY rate of 6.50, i.e., the NDF contract rate.

2. If the fixing rate on the fixing date is more favourable to ABC than the contract rate, ABC will pay the bank the cash settlement in USD on the maturity date.

So, say the fixing rate for USD/CNY is 6.76, the fixing settlement amount will be:

USD 1,479,289.94 (CNY 10,000,000/6.76)

While the contract settlement amount will be:

USD 1,538,461.54 (CNY 10,000,000/6.50)

The difference of USD 59,171.60 will be paid by ABC to the bank on the maturity date.

The cash settlement amount ABC pays the bank will reduce the extent to which ABC would have benefited through the lower USD amount when ABC paid for the goods. To purchase the goods, ABC pays USD 1,479,289.94. Adding the cash settlement amount (USD 59,171.60) ABC's total USD outlay will now be USD 1,538,461.54. This is equivalent to a USD/CNY exchange rate of 6.50, i.e., the NDF contract rate.

Entering into an NDF has effectively removed the uncertainty of fluctuations in the USD/CNY exchange rate on the USD amount that must be paid for the goods.

5. SWAP

A foreign exchange swap is an agreement to make an initial exchange of currencies for spot value with a reversal of that exchange at some future date. It differs from a forward outright in that two deliveries take place. Note that the flows of a swap are similar to borrowing one currency (the currency bought at spot) and investing another (the currency sold at spot). The exposure is therefore one of interest rate differential risk rather than currency (spot) risk. Swap trading is trading based upon how the interest rate differential is expected to move. Consequently, a bank will only charge (or pay) the interest differential. The price of the swap is therefore expressed in points (also referred to as forward points).

Advantages of a swap

- no spot exchange rate risk
- in comparison to the money market equivalent of borrowing one currency and investing another, the swap is, for corporate clients, an off balance sheet item
- low cost through avoiding borrowing margins
- by doing a swap rather than a separate spot and forward transaction the spread between the bid and offer is saved.

Uses of a swap

- the customer can switch currency assets and enhance yield on a fully hedged basis
- the customer can fund a borrowing requirement in one currency if running long balances in another at a cheaper rate by avoiding the margin
- the customer can switch any borrowing advantage it may have in one particular currency into the currency required
- banks use the spot and swap contracts to provide clients with a forward outright rate
- one can take a view on relative interest rate moves by varying the period
- clients can roll a position if, for example, receipts are late, contracts are delayed, etc.

How a swap is quoted

Swaps are quoted as two numbers and in our first example these are 145/144. When we quote a normal spot or forward outright price the left-hand side is the bid and the right-hand side is the offer (or ask). For a swap the opposite applies: 145 is the offer (the market maker sells and buys GBP), 144 is the bid (the market maker buys and sells GBP). As the points determine the price of the swap the spot rate used on the transaction is less important, although it must approximate to the current market price. The amount of one currency in a swap is normally held constant. Thus, the same amount of currency is bought spot as is sold forward. Mismatches though can easily be accommodated by buying or selling the difference at spot.

Table 6.13 shows a customer view of a swap.

Table 6.13 – Customer view of a swap

Offer	Bid
145	144
Buy GBP (Spot) & Sell GBP (Fwd) (Borrow GBP)	Sell GBP (Spot) & Buy GBP (Fwd) (Lend GBP)
Sell USD (Spot) & Buy USD (Fwd) (Lend USD)	Buy USD (Spot) & Sell USD (Fwd) (Borrow USD)
Interest rate – Pays away	Interest rate – Earns

Example of a customer swap transaction

We are now back at the dealing desk and ABC Plc is about to come on and ask for a six-month GBP/USD (cable) swap in GBP 2m. Spot GBP/USD is 1.4365 and today is 21 May. The swap is 145/144 in the market.

John from ABC – "Hi, John here from ABC. I need a six-month cable (GBP/USD) swap in GBP 2m. Can I have a price please?"

Dealer bank sales – "John, spot six-month?"

John from ABC – "Yes."

Dealer bank sales – "Spot six-month points are 145/144."

John from ABC – "OK, at 144 I sell and buy GBP 2m, 23 May vs. 23 November. Spot reference?"

Dealer bank sales – "1.4365."

John from ABC – "OK, ABC Plc sells and buys GBP 2m vs. USD, 1.4365/1.4221, 23 May vs. 23 November."

Dealer bank sales – "Agreed."

Looking at the cash flows:

- 1st delivery: ABC sells GBP 2,000,000 at 1.4365 and receives USD 2,873,000.

- 2nd delivery: ABC receives GBP 2,000,000 at 1.4221 (1.4365 - 0.0145) and sells USD 2,844,200.

In this example, ABC makes a net gain on the dollars – ABC earns through the swap. It is interest rate differentials that ABC will focus on and they would have to decide whether the swap price provided reflects this. The spot has a secondary role in the transaction, unlike in a forward outright where it is key.

Swap transactions – worked examples

Example 1 – GBP/USD

- Bank quotes one year swap at 324/321
- Date: 9/11/2002
- GBP/USD 1.5582
- Interest differential between GBP and USD is 2.1%

This example illustrates a crucial element of the swap – there is no foreign exchange exposure. In other words, there is no profit or loss if the spot rate moves up or down. I have shown some extreme moves in the spot to illustrate this point. The principal issue is the interest rate differential between sterling and dollars. For simplicity, the interest differential has been kept constant throughout the period at 2.1%.

The customer has sterling cash and wishes to fund a US property development on a fully hedged basis, i.e., with no foreign exchange exposure. The dollar requirement is USD 3m. The customer buys and sells USD 3m (sells and buys sterling) for one year, and then does the same for the next year. The period chosen was to take maximum advantage of the interest differential between the USD and GBP. There is a net interest gain, which over the period of the transaction amounts to GBP 214,658.99.

Movements in the spot exchange rate are only important in so far as they impact on cash flow. This is fine in the early years in the example when cash flow was positive but negative flows seen in the later years will have to be funded. This is an important consideration when evaluating a long-term transaction of this type.

The year-by-year transactions are shown in Table 6.14. In this example the flows are from the customer viewpoint.

Table 6.14 – Swap transactions year by year

Dates	Buy/ sell	Amount (USD)	Rate	Buy/ Sell	Amount (GBP)	Interest	Cash flow
11/09/2002	Buy	3,000,000	1.5582	Sell	1,925,298.42		
11/09/2003	Sell	3,000,000	1.5261	Buy	1,965,795.16	40,496.74	
11/09/2003	Buy	3,000,000	1.5421	Sell	1,945,399.13		1,965,795.16 - 1,945,399.13 = 20,396.03
11/09/2004	Sell	3,000,000	1.51	Buy	1,986,754.97	41,355.84	
11/09/2004	Buy	3,000,000	1.5721	Sell	1,908,275.55		1,986,754.97 - 1,908,275.55 = 78,479.42
11/09/2005	Sell	3,000,000	1.54	Buy	1,948,051.95	39,776.40	
11/09/2005	Buy	3,000,000	1.5021	Sell	1,997,203.91		1,948,051.95 - 1,997,203.91 = -49,151.96
11/09/2006	Sell	3,000,000	1.47	Buy	2,040,816.33	43,612.42	
11/09/2006	Buy	3,000,000	1.4121	Sell	2,124,495.43		2,040,816.33 - 2,124,495.43 = -83,679.11
11/09/2007	Sell	3,000,000	1.38	Buy	2,173,913.04	49,417.61	
Totals					248,614.62	214,659.01	-33,955.61

You may think that the final gain was GBP 248,614.62 as GBP 1,925,298.42 was sold on 11/09/2002 and GBP 2,173,913.04 was received on 11/09/2007 at the end of the process. However, you have to take into consideration the negative cumulative cash flow of GBP 33,955.61.

So, the net gain is:

GBP 248,614.62 - GBP 33,955.61 = GBP 214,659.01

This corresponds to the net interest received total, as shown in the table. The major risk is the interest rate differential. In money market terms, the customer is lending GBP and borrowing USD. If USD interest rates rise above GBP interest rates there will now be an interest rate cost. The customer may at any time decide to take on foreign exchange exposure by simply selling GBP and buying USD 3m for the next forward date.

The customer could have approached this another way. They could have arranged a back-to-back loan with their UK clearer. They would then place the GBP on deposit and borrow USD at 1% over the London interbank lending rate. While the swap will have an element of transaction costs, these will normally be relatively small, and the customer will be effectively borrowing close to the London interbank lending rate. A margin of 1% or more on borrowing, even cash-secured, would not be exceptional and in this circumstance the gain on the interest differential would be reduced if using a back-to-back loan.

Also, there may be tax to pay on the deposit, again reducing the benefit. How interest income and borrowing costs are treated will depend on the customer's tax situation. A back-to-back arrangement (unlike the swap) is on balance sheet and may have implications for borrowing ratios and lending covenants which need to be addressed in advance.

Example 2

On 3 April a customer has surplus cash in his USD account but is overdrawn in his GBP account. This situation is expected to last for six months (185 days). The customer can borrow GBP at 4.32% and lend USD at 2.25% for six months in the money markets.

They sell USD 1m for spot delivery and simultaneously agree to buy back USD 1m, six months forward (7 October).

The GBP/USD spot rate is 1.4365; the six month forward points are 145/144. As explained earlier, the customer will deal at -145.

First delivery: The customer sells USD 1m at 1.4365 and receives GBP 696,136.44, spot value 5 April. The overdraft is cleared.

Second delivery: The customer buys USD 1m at 1.4220 and pays GBP 703,234.88 value 7 October (six months forward).

The net GBP cost is:

GBP 703,234.88 - GBP 696,136.44 = GBP 7,098.44

This represents an interest differential of 2.01%.

GBP 703,234.88 - GBP 696,136.44 = GBP 7,098.44

GBP 7,098.44/GBP 696,136.44 x 365/185 = 2.01%

To show the borrowing cost in GBP I add this differential to the USD deposit rate of 2.25%. However, USD interest and GBP interest are calculated using different day counts. USD is calculated actual days/360, GBP actual days/365. So the USD interest rate in GBP terms is 2.25% x 365/360 = 2.28%. This represents a GBP borrowing cost of: 2.01% + (2.25% x 365/360) = 4.29%.

In this example there is a net interest cost and the forward points (-145) fully reflect this.

However, the main advantage of this tactic is that it avoids the borrowing margin on the sterling and there is no spot risk. It may also free up the borrowing facility for other requirements. Another advantage for companies of the money market equivalent of borrowing one currency and investing another is that a swap is an off balance sheet item.

Example 3a – improving yield using the swap, fully hedged

Mr Smith wishes to improve his sterling return. In this instance this can be achieved through the purchase of dollar commercial paper with a six-month maturity using the swap without incurring an exchange rate risk. Table 6.15 shows the details of this transaction.

Table 6.15 – A six-month swap used to improve the pound deposit rate

GBP/USD swap points	145/144
Spot	1.4365
Forward	1.4365 - 0.0144 = 1.4221
Period: six months 5 April to 7 October	185 days
Pound deposit interest rate	4.25%
Dollar yield on commercial paper	2.35%
Sell GBP 5m at 1.4365	USD 7,182,500
Interest (2.35% x USD 7,182,500 x 185/360)	USD 86,738.66
Principal + interest	USD 7,182,500 + USD 86,738.66 = USD 7,269,238.66

When Mr Smith sells back the USD 7,269,238.66 and buys pounds he receives GBP 5,111,622.71 (USD 7,269,238.66/1.4221). He has earned GBP 111,622.71 from the swap (GBP 5,111,622.71 - GBP 5,000,000).

Therefore, his effective sterling return is:

111,622.71/5,000,000 x 365/185 = 4.4%

Mr Smith has thus improved upon the pound deposit rate of 4.25% by achieving an effective deposit rate of 4.4%.

Example 3b – capital growth scenario

Mr Smith has surplus cash in his GBP account. He wishes to invest in a US hedge fund without incurring an exchange rate risk. US hedge funds are usually USD-based but some institutions will offer this product in GBP. In other words, they will operate the swap process on the customer's behalf. The forward date would normally correspond to the redemption date, which is in six months' time. In this case Mr Smith enters into a swap, selling GBP spot with a simultaneous agreement to buy back in six months' time.

The advantages of this are:

- no spot risk
- flexibility to create a spot position if this becomes an advantageous move
- exposure only to relative interest rates (USD vs. GBP)

- easy to adjust for growth in US investment (simply sell more USD forward).

The disadvantages are:

- It may have been more profitable to have had a spot exposure at the outset, i.e., to sell GBP and buy USD. GBP/USD traded at the extreme 1.90/2.10 for a number of years.

- Exposure to relative interest rates needs to be monitored, especially if the investment is not performing well. If GBP interest rates are higher than USD interest rates, they will gain by the interest rate differential. However, if that relationship reverses then they will need to assess whether that swap loss is acceptable against the investment return.

Example 4

In 2010 there were a number of occasions (especially at the end of months and quarters) when US dollar money market funding was proving extremely difficult for European banks. With difficulties to obtain USD in the straight cash market, European banks utilised the liquid EUR/USD foreign exchange swap market to produce USD from EUR. The European banks sold EUR for USD spot and bought them back for an agreed period, which in this instance was six months. Inevitably this raised the price of USD.

Clearly if borrowers of USD were being forced to pay more via the swap this opened the door for lenders to improve the yield on their deposits by utilising the swap. Here is an actual example that was dealt from the end of May 2010. Customers were only receiving 0.79% in a six-month USD deposit but by executing the swap selling USD the effective USD interest was increased to over 1.24%. The EUR received were placed on deposit at 0.88% for six months. Table 6.16 shows the details of this trade.

Table 6.16 – EUR/USD swap used to earn a better interest rate

	Buy (EUR)	Spot rate	Sell (USD)
Spot leg	50,000,000	1.2331	61,655,000
Lend EUR at	0.88		
Effective interest USD yield			1.2645942
Normal USD yield			0.79
Yield pickup (bps)			0.47
Number of days			183
Swap points		0.0024	
	Sell EUR (P+I)	Forward rate	Buy USD (P+I)
Forward leg	50,223,666.67	1.2355	62,051,340.17
Interest exposure (EUR)	223,666.67		

Note: the EUR interest will need to be sold (hedged).

Option 1

Customer A has surplus USD 61,655,000 which they could place on deposit for six months (183 days). Interest at maturity would be:

USD 61,655,000 x 0.79% x 183/360 = USD 247,596.20

Principal plus interest = USD 61,902,596.20.

Option 2 (summarised in Table 6.16)

Customer A enters into a EUR/USD swap; they buy EUR 50m, sell USD 61,655,000 at 1.2331 spot value and agree to sell EUR (principal + interest) in six months' time at a rate of 1.2355 (1.2331 + 0.0024).

EUR interest = EUR 50,000,000 x 0.88% x 183/360 = 223,666.67

It is assumed that the interest is sold at the outset, otherwise customer A will have spot risk on this amount.

USD proceeds in six months:

EUR 50,223,666.67 at 1.2355 = USD 62,051,340.17

This is USD 148,743.97 more than if it was placed on a straight USD deposit (USD 62,051,340.17 - USD 61, 902,596.20).

Customer A receives net USD 396,340.17. To work out the interest return the calculation is:

(USD 396,340.17/USD 61,655,000) x (360/183) x 100

This equates to a return of 1.26%, a gain of about 0.47 bps (USD 148,743.97).

Example 5 – saving the financial system

In December 2007 the US Federal Reserve established swap lines to central banks. The dollar swap facilities were set up to improve liquidity conditions in global (and US) financial markets by providing foreign central banks with the capacity to deliver US dollar funding to institutions in their jurisdiction which in turn should lower borrowing rates. The normal interbank funding market had ceased to function as banks became increasingly uncertain over bank credit risk in general and to their own short-term cash needs. There was a shortage of dollars and this was evident in a sharp rise in borrowing rates. The emphasis on the dollar is essentially due to its pre-eminence as a funding currency within its role as the major reserve currency.

When a foreign bank draws on its swap facility with the Federal Reserve the foreign central bank sells a specified amount of its currency to the Federal Reserve in exchange for dollars at the prevailing market exchange rate. The Federal Reserve holds the foreign currency in an account at the foreign central bank.

The dollars that the Federal Reserve provides are deposited in an account that the foreign central bank maintains at the Federal Reserve Bank of New York. At the same time the parties contract to swap back these currencies at a specified date in the future, which is the next day or as far as three months, using the same exchange rate as in the initial transaction. As movements in the exchange rate did not alter the eventual payments these swap operations carried no exchange rate risk.

As we have seen, in a typical swap, interest differential is accounted for at the outset through the swap point adjustment. In the Federal Reserve arrangement the spot and the forward rates are the same and interest is settled at the maturity of the second transaction. The foreign central bank distributed the dollars through a variety of methods such as variable rate tenders, fixed-rate tenders and bilateral transactions and these were against various forms of collateral. At the programme's peak, in the week ending 10 December 2008, swaps outstanding were over USD 580bn.

Example 6a – late receipts

ABC Company is to receive USD 5m in royalties from its Christmas sales. Royalties are paid three months after 15 January on 15 April. The ABC board decided to hedge this receipt given market volatility at the time. They decide to sell the dollars for sterling for value on 15 April at the inspirational rate of 1.35. They now have an obligation to deliver dollars for which they will receive sterling.

Unfortunately, in February they receive news that the audit of the sales is to be delayed by a month and as a result they will not receive the dollar payment until 15 May.

The first decision is to inform the bank. There are a number of options. The forward outright rate is now at 1.65 so ABC Company could close out the hedge at a nice profit.

ABC - USD 5m + GBP at 1.35 = GBP 3,703,703

ABC + USD 5m - GBP at 1.65 = GBP 3,030,303

Profit = GBP 3,703,703 - GBP 3,030,303 = GBP 673,400

This operation of course could be executed at anytime up to 15 April but it does leave the receivable dollars unhedged.

The second option is to wait until 15 April and then borrow the dollars. On 15 April, ABC dollar account will be debited USD 5m and their sterling account will be credited GBP 3,703,703.

There are a number of possible drawbacks to this. The first of these is cost, as it is likely any borrowing will have the bank's margin attached. Also, this borrowing may restrict ABC's ability to borrow other sums elsewhere. ABC will receive sterling which will attract interest, so this is a compensating factor.

The third option, and the one generally favoured, is to roll the transaction via a foreign exchange swap to 15 May. ABC could have executed a window forward at the outset of the transaction to take account of the possibility that the royalty payment might be delayed.

Example 6b – early receipts

As well as being delayed, funds can also be received early. If this were the case for ABC, with their royalty payment of USD 5m as discussed in Example 6a, they could sit on the dollars until the maturity of the forward contract or they could execute a swap. Intuitively one can easily assess whether there is a cost involved by looking at the interest rates on the two currencies. If the currency with the higher interest rate is received early this is clearly to the advantage of the customer and to the disadvantage of the bank. However, the rate provided by the bank will take account of this.

Let's say ABC has received the USD 5m royalties on 13 March and decides to settle the contract early. The bank agrees to bring the contract forward to settle for spot value on 15 March. The bank is under no obligation to do this but normally would.

The forward points for the period 15 March to 15 April are 24/23. As we saw earlier, this indicates that sterling interest rates are higher than dollars. Spot is now priced at 1.65.

Initial contract: ABC sells USD 5m and buys GBP 3,703,703 15/4 at a rate of 1.35.

As part of the swap, ABC needs to sell USD 5m spot and buy USD 5m for 15 April. Remember that this will be based on the current spot, which is 1.65.

With the GBP/USD swap quoted as 24/23, ABC will deal at -24, which makes the forward leg of the swap 1.6476 (1.6500 - 0.0024). ABC sells USD 5m value 15 March at 1.6500 and buys USD 5m value 15 April at 1.6476. Table 6.17 shows ABC's cash flow.

Table 6.17 – Cash flow for ABC

15 March	- USD 5m	+ GBP 3, 030,303 at 1.65
15 April	+ USD 5m	- GBP 3,034,717 at 1.6476
15 April	- USD 5m	+ GBP 3,703,703 at 1.35

By receiving GBP earlier, ABC will benefit from higher GBP interest rates vs. USD and will compensate the bank through the swap, which accounts for this interest rate differential. In this example the swap cost is GBP 4,414 (GBP 3,034,717 - GBP 3,030,303).

On 15 April there is positive cash flow for ABC of GBP 672,986 (GBP 3,707,703 - GBP 3,034,717). This should not be confused as profit as their proceeds will not have changed. They have still dealt at 1.35 (minus swap cost) but receives this positive cash flow as on 15 March (the first leg of the swap) they will be dealing at 1.6500.

Example 7 – trading forwards/swaps

In Example 1 above I assumed the interest differential was constant at 2.1%. This is rarely the case of course. The one year swap was 324/321 and this approximates to an interest differential between GBP and USD of 2.1% (sterling interest rates are higher than dollars).

If the bank dealer thinks this interest gap will narrow then they will sell the swap. In this example they will trade at -321, which means that they will sell and buy sterling (buy and sell dollars).

I have assumed both selling and buying trades (cover) are executed on the same day and the movement in the swap price is quite dramatic.

In the first covering example the spot is the same as the original trade but the swap points have moved from -321 to -100, a profit of 221 points. The original trade was to sell and buy sterling (buy and sell dollars); the cover trade will buy and sell sterling (sell and buy dollars). This generates a profit of GBP 28,061.04 (GBP 40,496.74 - GBP 12,435.70).

Using a different spot rate for the covering trade (as in the second covering example) will impact on cash flow. Positive cash flow is lent for the period and negative cash flow would need to be borrowed. When this is taken into account the overall result is broadly the same.

The details of these covering trades are shown in Table 6.18.

Table 6.18 – Cover trade examples. GBP/USD is 1.5582. Date 9/11/2002

Dates	Buy/ sell	Amount (USD)	Rate	Buy/ sell	Amount (GBP)	Interest	Profit
11/9/2002	+	3,000,000	1.5582	-	1,925,298.42		
11/9/2003	-	3,000,000	1.5261	+	1,965,795.16	40,496.74	
Cover trade example one							
11/9/2002	-	3,000,000	1.5582	+	1,925,298.42		
11/9/2003	+	3,000,000	1.5482	-	1,937,734.14	-12,435.70	28,061.04
Cover trade example two							
11/9/2002	-	3,000,000	1.5721	+	1,908,275.55		
11/9/2003	+	3,000,000	1.5621	-	1,920,491.65	-12,216.10	28,280.64

In practice the position may have to run for a period to meet the trader's target. It is important to remember that the trader has to fund the position. They have sold GBP and bought USD spot. Therefore, they will need to do a covering trade. This may be run on an overnight swap or whatever period fits their view on interest rates.

How a bank covers a position

When a customer deals with a bank there is in effect a transfer of risk. The customer is selling their foreign exchange risk to the bank. With the execution of a spot trade the bank is at risk from movements in the spot exchange rate and with the execution of a forward outright the bank is at risk from movements in the spot exchange rate and movements in the interest rate differential between the two currencies. Let's take an example using the following figures:

- Spot GBP/USD: 1.6171/1.6177

- Swap three-month points: 104/103

The customer wishes to buy USD 1m forward for settlement in three months' time. The bank would quote 1.6067 (1.6171 - 0.0104). Therefore, the bank sells USD 1m and buys GBP 622,393.73 for settlement in three months' time.

The bank's position is short USD 1m and long GBP 622,393.72 but the bank's cash position will not reflect this until three months' time when it will receive sterling from the client into its account and pay away to the customer USD 1m.

There are a number of ways that the bank could deal with this:

- *First solution*: Do nothing until the value date becomes a spot date and then make a spot trade in the market to buy USD 1m at the prevailing rate and sell the equivalent amount of sterling. This is a very high risk strategy as it leaves the bank with a position for three months and a very uncertain profit or loss.

- *Second solution*: Obtain a quote from another bank to exactly match the customer trade. If we assume the customer was dealing at interbank prices and these prices were unchanged, the bank's dealing position would be cleared (squared up) as would also be the cash position in three months' time.

Therefore trades going through in three months' time would be as shown in Table 6.19.

Table 6.19 – Bank's trades in three months' time

Original trade (with customer)	- USD 1m	+ GBP 622,393.72
Cover trade (with another bank)	+ USD 1m	- GBP 622,393.72
Overall position	0	0

While this appears to be an elegant solution and is easily achievable with dealing platforms it does not offer any profit. The key issues here are the risk appetite for the bank and on what terms the bank is prepared to price the customer trades.

If the bank quotes a lower rate to the customer and then covers then there is an immediate profit; if not, the bank is reliant on a favourable exchange rate move or another customer trading the opposite way. Another customer making an opposite trade would then provide the bank with a dealing spread profit (difference between bid and offer/ask). This illustrates the need for banks to have volume in order to generate income.

- *Third solution*: Use the money market. Immediately after the three-month forward trade is executed with the customer the bank could make a spot foreign exchange transaction. The details of this approach are shown in Table 6.20.

Table 6.20 – Solution using the money market

Original trade	- USD 1m	+ GBP 622,393.72
Spot trade	+ USD 1m	- GBP 618,390.94
Overall position	0	+ USD 4,002.78

While the bank's dealing position in foreign exchange has been covered there is a timing difference with the cash. The bank will receive USD 1m for spot value that will not be needed for three months, while in the sterling account an overdraft will occur.

To resolve this the dollars could be lent in the money markets for three months and the sterling borrowed in the money markets for three months.

The profit to the bank would be determined by:

- profit on foreign exchange (difference between spot and forward rates)
- income on dollars for three months
- cost of borrowing sterling for three months.

The net result in this example should be zero. The gain between the spot and forward rates should equate to the interest differential between the two currencies.

- *Fourth solution*: Use the swap foreign exchange market. This is the most common method. The third solution above involved borrowing and lending in the money market. In other words, balance sheet items (asset/liability) were created. The bank may not wish to expand its balance sheet in this manner.

As in the third solution, a spot foreign exchange trade is dealt to cover the foreign exchange position. By doing this the dealer has created a swap position. This generally presents far less risk than a straight spot foreign exchange position.

- Spot GBP/USD: 1.6171/1.6177
- Swap three-month points: 104/103

The customer buys USD 1m forward for settlement in three months' time at 1.6067 (1.6171 - 0.0104):

- Bank: Spot + USD 1m - GBP at 1.6171
- Customer: three months - USD 1m + GBP at 1.6067

The bank has + USD 1m spot and - USD 1m three months; a swap has been created.

The bank will now have to trade a swap to cover. The bank will sell USD 1m spot and buy USD 1m three months.

The final picture from the bank's perspective:

Bank: Spot + USD 1m - GBP at 1.6171. Customer: Three months - USD 1m + GBP at 1.6067. Bank Swap: Spot - USD 1m +GBP ; three months + USD 1m - GBP.

The maturity dates of the customer's and bank's swaps do not necessarily have to match as the bank dealer may have a view on interest rates and will again use the swap to manage the cash position.

Bank positions – long and short

To facilitate international transactions a bank will maintain accounts in a range of foreign currencies with either their overseas branches or with other banks. Such accounts are called *nostro* or *due from* accounts. Balances will be left in these accounts and these represent a foreign exchange exposure to the bank and a loss of interest. As a rule, these accounts maintained with foreign correspondents must not be overdrawn. Such credit balances are foreign exchange assets and thus they are long positions. Since these foreign currencies had to be bought with another currency – often the bank's domestic currency – the bank is automatically short its domestic currency.

It is not just these balances which make up the foreign exchange position of a bank. The position also includes the difference between outstanding foreign exchange contracts for both spot and forward delivery. There is also the difference between interest to be received in a foreign currency and interest to be paid away in the same foreign currency. These represent the major daily exposures. There may be a long-term investment abroad which has not been covered by a foreign currency borrowing or a forward exchange contract; these may not be considered for the daily dealing purpose.

Finally, other payables or receivables in foreign currencies would include taxes, fees, dividends, etc. Every day a revaluation rate would be applied to each of the currency exposures. The position is measured on a net basis and would be expressed in the bank's own domestic currency. The size of position that can be held will vary from bank to bank and will depend on the size and market activity of the bank, and to some extent on the level of expertise of the bank concerned. It is usually monitored in real time from the risk department.

6. FORWARD/FORWARD

A forward/forward is the purchase (sale) of one currency against another for a future date and the sale (purchase) of the same currency against another for a further future date.

Up until this point the examples used have shown positions that have conveniently been covered exactly by the dealers. In practice mismatches (settlement differences) occur regularly, although the overall foreign exchange position could show zero. For example, in Table 6.21 the dealer's uncovered position is zero. For simplicity I have used a constant GBP/USD exchange rate.

Table 6.21 – A dealer's overall position equating to zero, despite settlement differences

	GBP	USD
Spot	-	-
Three months	-2,500,000	+4,000,000
Six months	+4,000,000	-6,400,000
Twelve months	-1,500,000	+2,400,000
Overall position	0	0

There are three ways in which to close out these gaps.

1. Execute a series of swaps, spot, three-month, spot six-month, spot twelve-month in the opposite direction (equal and opposite transactions).

2. Find a counterparty to trade forward/forward. In the example this would be a trade three-month versus six-month and six-month versus twelve-month.

3. Lend and borrow.

We will now look at the second of these choices – trading forward/forward – in more detail.

Forward/forward quotes

The important thing to remember is that unlike a normal swap, which starts from spot, the forward/forward will start at a date in the future and a swap adjustment needs to be made for this period. Below I have taken a quote (only one side of the price, for simplicity) from a dealing platform. It is notable how many decimal places they will go to.

Example

- Spot GBP/USD on 3/11/10: 1.6075

- three-month (3/2/11) points: -13.15

- six-month (3/5/11) points: -29.72

The forward/forward three-month versus six-month price will be quoted 1.606185 (1.6075 - 0.001315) for value 3/2/11 and 1.604528 (1.6075 - 0.002972) for valve 3/5/11.

The forward/forward swap is 0.001657 (1.606185 - 1.604528).

Forward/swap mismatches

On occasions the swap amounts can be different between the spot and the forward. For example, in GBP/USD the customer buys USD 10m spot and sells USD 10.3m in six months' time. The bank will normally cover in even amounts. In this case the bank would choose USD 10.3m but they will be left with a small spot exposure which is easily managed.

Customer (bank view)

- - USD 10m + GBP spot

- + USD 10.3m - GBP six months

Bank cover

- Swap + USD 10.3m - GBP spot

- - USD 10.3m + GBP six months

- Spot + USD 0.3m - GBP spot

Normally the setting of the spot is not important but as a spot position has been created by the cover, the bank will need to take this into account. In this case the bank will need to buy USD 0.3m and sell GBP and will mark the spot higher.

Forwards and the carry trade

The carry trade is borrowing in low-interest currencies, converting these to other currencies and then using the monies to invest in assets such as property, equities, commodities and bonds. I shall be covering carry trades later in more detail (see chapter 11) but it is useful to see how a forward could be used to take the spot risk out of the carry trade. Many who are involved in the carry trade utilise three-month borrowings or longer and are not aware that they can remove the spot risk prior to the maturity of the loan through a forward.

Example of using a forward with a carry trade

A client has a UK property portfolio with GBP 1m of borrowing and sees cheaper funding in USD. The client borrows USD and converts to GBP to repay the loan. In this case the client sells USD 1.6m at 1.6 to produce GBP 1m. The details of this trade are shown in Table 6.22.

Table 6.22 – Using a forward with a carry trade

Amount	GBP 1m
Borrowing costs three months	USD 0.51%, GBP 0.85%
Period	92 days
Spot GBP/USD	1.6
Forward three months	12.7/12.3
Interest cost if borrowing taken in GBP	GBP 2,142.47 (GBP 1m x 0.85% x 92/365)
Interest cost of borrowing taken in USD	USD 2,085.33 (USD 1.6m x 0.51% x 92/360)

If the exchange rate stays the same over the three-month period the client will have saved 0.34% (0.85% - 0.51%). If the spot rate moves to 1.7 at the maturity this is good news as this will mean that they only require GBP 942,403.11 to repay the USD borrowing (including interest).

However, if the spot has moved to 1.5 there is loss to deal with; they will need GBP 1,068,056.80 to repay the USD borrowing. The borrower has taken on spot risk for an improvement in borrowing costs. Rather than waiting until the loan maturity to revert back to GBP borrowing, they could achieve this through a forward. To reinforce the point they decide to do this straightaway.

They will sell GBP and buy dollars three months forward. If they left it to the maturity date of the USD loan then they would have to borrow GBP and sell sufficient to repay the USD principal and interest. The three-month forward rate is 1.59873 (1.6 - 0.00127). The GBP amount would be GBP 1,002,098.75 ((USD 1,600,000 + USD 2,085.33)/1.59873), which is nearly the same as what it would have cost the client if the borrowing was in GBP (GBP 1,000,000 + GBP 2,142.47 = GBP 1,002,142.47). The interest rate differential was reflected in the forward points. Of course it would be more likely that this trade would be done a while into the period of the loan, prompted possibly by the extreme price moves in the example.

In this type of trade there is no gain without the risk of loss but losses in this instance can be contained via a forward. Failure to recognise this proved extremely costly for many in the trade 2008/09. Also, many investments were only viable when financed by low rates of interest.

Hedging

Single Farm Payments (SFPs)

This was introduced on 1 January 2005 as part of a package to reform the Common Agricultural Policy and to remove the link between subsidies and production of specific crops. Under EU legislation the payment of SFP for 2011 must be made during the period 1 December 2011 to 30 June 2012. Up to 80% of payments should be completed by 31 January 2012.

The landowner can elect to be paid either in GBP or EUR. However, the entitlements are in EUR and the rate to be used to convert payments from EUR to GBP is set by the EU on 30 September of each scheme year. Once a request has been made to be paid in EUR, it is not possible to revert to payment in GBP for that scheme year. Either way the landowner is exposed to the movements in EUR/GBP. The various hedging options are shown below. The landowner can of course do nothing.

SFP receipts in GBP

Process

The farmer enters into a forward contract to sell EUR and buy GBP on 30 September. On 30 September the farmer will instruct the bank to close out the trade. This is by transacting an equal and opposite trade at the prevailing rate in the market because the farmer does not yet have any EUR to sell.

The farmer will either realise a profit, which will make up for any disadvantage after the SFP setting, or a loss, to be realised against an advantage made after the SFP rate setting. While these should be similar to the SFP conversion rate, it is unlikely to be exactly the same, as rates fluctuate during the day, and there is a spread between buying and selling rates. To illustrate the process, however, I assumed that the rates are the same.

Example

Assume SFP due is EUR 100,000.

Current spot rate is EUR/GBP 0.90.

Forward rate to sell EUR 100,000 on 30 September is 0.90.

To fix the value of the SFP the farmer will contract to sell EUR 100, 000 to the bank on 30/9 and receive GBP 90,000.

On 30/9 the farmer closes out his maturing contract by buying EUR 100, 000 and selling GBP at the prevailing rate.

Scenario 1

If the prevailing rate is 0.95 on 30/9 there is a loss of GBP 5000.

The flows are: farmer sells EUR 100, 000 and buys GBP 90,000 (0.9).

The farmer buys EUR 100,000 and sells GBP 95,000 (0.95).

The SFP due is EUR 100,000 at the rate set on 30/9 of 0.95, which will be GBP 95,000.

The farmer receives GBP 95,000 SFP which, after the trading loss of GBP 5000, is GBP 90,000 providing an effective rate of 0.9.

Scenario 2

If on 30/9 the rate has fallen to 0.85 then there is a profit of GBP 5000.

The flows are: farmer sells EUR 100, 000 and buys GBP 90,000 (0.90).

The farmer buys EUR 100,000 and sells GBP 85,000.

The SFP due is EUR 100,000 at the rate set on 30/9 of 0.85, which will be GBP 85,000.

The farmer receives GBP 85,000 SFP which, after the trading profit of GBP 5000, is GBP 90,000.

No matter what the prevailing rates are on 30/9 the net receipt will be GBP 90,000, which is an effective rate 0.90.

SFP receipts in EUR

Enter into a window forward contract

The farmer can enter into a *window forward* or *time option forward* to sell EUR 100,000 at any time between two dates.

Enter into a forward outright contract

The farmer can enter into a forward contract to sell EUR 100,000 for 1 December. If there is no receipt the contract can be rolled via a foreign exchange swap.

A further application – hedging bonuses or income linked to an exchange rate setting in the future

Some US law and accountancy firms will pay bonuses to UK staff determined by the GBP/USD exchange rate prevailing on a particular date in the future. However, the entitlement is set in USD and will be paid some months after this date. Exactly the same process utilised for the SFP can be used to hedge. In this case, USD will be sold forward to the rate setting date and on this date an equal and opposite trade will be executed. This, as in the case of the SFP, will generate a profit and loss to set against the conversion rate.

Summary

In summary, the main uses of forwards are as follows:

- hedging – tactic to offset losses or potential losses; a perfect hedge eliminates the possibility of future loss or gain

- to eliminate uncertainty

- to preserve margins:

  - in trade, to cover export receivables or import payables

  - in finance, if income is predominantly paid in a foreign currency on a periodic basis and expenses are in your domestic currency, e.g., hedge funds, research companies based in the UK

- to protect foreign investments, e.g., share or bond portfolio

- to trade for profit.

The advantages of forwards are that they are simple, cheap and flexible, especially when compared to options, which are explained in detail later.

7. ALGORITHMIC TRADING

Algorithmic trading – otherwise known as 'high frequency trading', 'automated trading', or 'black-box trading' – is widely used by investment banks, hedge funds, pension funds and banks. An algorithmic trading system can be defined as any rule-based system systematically implemented via electronic trading with counterparties involving little or no human intervention.

In the past few years algorithmic trading has developed markedly in the foreign exchange markets. The growth in this area has been driven by four factors:

1. developments in computer power and electronic trading

2. high liquidity

3. virtual 24/7 trading

4. very low transaction costs.

Algorithmic trading can involve the working of an order (to buy or sell) to achieve the best execution, utilising various pricing sources (or 'liquidity pools', as they are often referred to). An algorithm programmed into a computer will decide on aspects such as the timing, the price, and even the final size of the order – the program makes the decisions based on information that is received electronically. It can also simply aim to trade for profit from different pricing across liquidity pools and arbitrage, or simply speculation.

A simple example of a high frequency trade is to produce a system that automatically buys EUR 30m if EUR/USD moves up 8 pips, and then automatically offers to sell 10 pips higher.

Such trading is usually carried out by sophisticated corporates and asset managers, many of whom already execute via algorithms in other asset classes such as equities and futures. For banks it will be used in interbank pricing. The major banks have developed electronic trading platforms which has facilitated the growth in this type of trading.

Trading models are developed for high or low frequency trading, which generate transactions that can then be traded via these electronic channels. This enables the algorithmic trader to access the market very quickly. This, coupled with reduced dealing spreads, has made a number of previously unprofitable strategies viable. The ultimate program merely translates events into numbers. Therefore emotion is no longer an issue, and shoal trading and inexplicable price action will become more prevalent.

The nature of the algorithmic trading is that it utilises high volume and low spreads, and so its potential weakness lies in liquidity. In volatile conditions there is not sufficient liquidity to support these trading models and they can therefore destabilise an already unstable market. This has yet to be fully addressed by the regulators but with model trading set to expand the regulators could take action sooner rather than later.

8. OPTIONS

For anyone looking to trade foreign exchange a knowledge of options is very important. I have not attempted to provide an exhaustive study of foreign exchange options here. This text is geared largely to the newcomer, although it will be of interest to companies wishing to hedge foreign exchange risk and experienced traders who are not directly involved in the options market. I have avoided the mathematics of options, which are extremely complex.

The relatively simple task of buying or selling an option hides a considerable amount of mathematical complexity in the pricing formulae which is beyond most customers. The majority of option users are therefore reliant on obtaining comparative quotes from a number of providers to ensure that pricing is accurate. This is not a problem for straightforward or vanilla style products but for complex, bespoke structures, for example those involving barriers, especially outside the major traded currencies, this is not always easily achieved.

Currency options – the basics

A currency option confers upon the buyer (holder) of the option the right but not the obligation to exchange a fixed amount of one currency in return for another currency at a fixed rate of exchange on an agreed date in the future. The essence of an option is that it is a right not an obligation. The holder of an option is not committed to an options contract as they would be to a forward contract. In addition, a key characteristic of options is that they can be used to hedge or trade currency volatility.

For example, take a UK company with revenues in US dollars. If the dollar strengthens against the pound sterling then revenues will increase and if the dollar weakens, sterling revenues will fall. The company might be happy with the upside potential but unwilling to accept the downside risk.

To deal with this the company will need to find a counterparty that is prepared to take on any potential losses from the exposure to GBP/USD in return for a fee. The company will buy an option contract. In this case the company would buy a USD put/ GBP call. For some, options are regarded as a type of insurance contract, reducing their exposure. For others, an option can be used to express a directional view on future exchange rates which represents taking on additional risk.

In consideration of receiving the option right the buyer pays to the seller (sometimes called 'the writer') a fee known as 'the premium'. The premium is normally paid two working days (spot) after dealing and represents the maximum that can be lost by the buyer and therefore represents the maximum profit to the seller. A seller of an option does have an obligation to buy or sell the asset if the owner of the option exercises it.

In its simplest form, buying an option is akin to taking a spot position with a stop loss. The maximum that can be lost is the premium.

The delivery (or maturity) date of an option is the date the foreign exchange cash position created by an option exercise is delivered. This delivery would be for value two working days (spot) from exercise date.

Calls and puts

An option can either be a *call*, which gives the right to buy a specified currency, or a *put*, which gives the right to sell a specified currency. As mentioned previously, in foreign exchange we are always dealing with two currencies. What this means for options is that a call on one currency has to be a put on the other currency within the pair. For example, in GBP/USD, a call on GBP is also a put on USD because the holder's right to buy GBP would result in them having to sell USD (in order to buy GBP). In view of this, the call and put currencies need to be clearly defined when entering into option transactions.

Strike price

The predetermined rate of exchange at which the exercise of an option takes place is known as 'the strike' or 'strike price'. This is the price at which the option purchaser has the right to buy the call currency (and sell the put currency). For instance, in GBP/USD, 'GBP call 1.6 strike' means the customer has the right to buy GBP 1 and sell USD 1.6 at expiry. The price (premium) of an option is very sensitive to the relationship of the strike to the spot rate.

Settlement of an option

The buyer of an option has the right to exercise the option (take delivery of the exchange) or not. If the decision is to take delivery the buyer must notify the seller of the decision.

Currency options are usually settled by the physical exchange of the underlying currencies, e.g., receive sterling and pay dollars. The physical exercise of this option is therefore effectively the cancellation of the option and the creation of a spot foreign exchange transaction. They may also be settled by the payment to the holder of the net difference between the strike price and the exchange rate on the expiry date. This is referred to as cash exercise.

Options are only exercised if it is beneficial to do so. It is unlikely that someone would exercise an option when the currency could be bought or sold at a better level on the prevailing spot market. Options that are not exercised expire worthless. An interesting statistic from exchange traded options is that around 80% expire worthless.

Important dates

- *Trade date*: the date the trade is done and strike, maturity, etc., set.

- *Value or start date*: the date that the option/options go live and when, if applicable, the option premium is paid.

- *Exercise date/time, Expiry date/time*: the date/time that the reference price is fixed to determine whether the option is exercised or not.

- *Maturity date/delivery date*: the date the foreign exchange cash position created by an option exercise is delivered (the final cash flows are paid or received). This delivery is usually set for value two working days (spot) from exercise date.

Different styles of option

The vast majority of options are written as European style, which means they may only be exercised at expiry. American style options allow exercise at any time during the life of the option. Another variation is an Asian option where the strike price is based on the average of the price of the underlying over the life of the option. Asian options are nearly always cheaper than conventional options because the averaging process reduces the volatility used for pricing the option and consequently reduces the premium of the option. Technically, the averaging process makes it easier to hedge the option as it becomes a portfolio of options with different maturity dates. The risk of markets moving wildly close to the exercise price near maturity is therefore spread out over multiple days. The style of option dealt is not a condition of location.

The expiration time of an option is generally 10 am New York time (New York cut) which is 1500 GMT apart from the week or so when there is the BST switch (in the last week of March and October). Options settled in Asia will use the Tokyo cut (10 am London). Cut-off time is the time of day on the expiry date by which point the owner of the option must exercise the option if he or she wishes.

The value of an option

The value of an option is the sum of the intrinsic value and time value.

Intrinsic value

Intrinsic value represents the value of an option if exercised. For American-style options this is the difference between the strike price and the underlying spot rate and for European-style options the difference between the strike price and the foreign exchange forward rate (or spot rate at expiry) multiplied by the face amount.

For example, consider a GBP call USD put European-style option with strike 1.6 with spot at 1.65 on the expiry date of the option.

The intrinsic value is USD 5 cents (1.65 - 1.6) and is positive because exercise of the option produces GBP at a lower level than the current market. In this case the option holder would almost certainly exercise the option.

If spot was 1.55 on the expiry date of this option there would be no positive intrinsic value as the holder could buy GBP at 1.55 in the market rather than at 1.6 through the option. In this case the option would expire worthless with no intrinsic value. Conversely, with the strike price at 1.6 and spot at 1.55 a GBP put option would be exercised due to its USD 5 cents intrinsic value. The premium of an option will reflect the full amount of any intrinsic value.

This has brought us to a point where we can look at three of the most important terms in options:

1.   An option that has intrinsic value is *in the money* (ITM).

2.   An option that has no intrinsic value is *out of the money* (OTM).

3.   An option where the strike is at the underlying foreign exchange rate is *at the money* (ATM).

Options which are OTM have no intrinsic value and are priced on their time value alone. Options ITM will have intrinsic value added to their time value.

It is important to note that to determine whether an option is ITM, ATM or OTM at any time before the expiry date of the option the strike must be compared with the forward rate, not the spot (European style options).

In some currency pairs where there is a large interest rate differential, the spot and the forward can be very different. What matters is where the spot is expected to be at expiry, i.e., the forward rate. An ITM option will be the most expensive. An OTM option will be the cheapest. An ATM option is the most commonly traded.

To summarise:

- A call (put) option is ITM if the forward price is above (below) the strike price, i.e., the option has intrinsic value.

- A call (put) option is ATM if the forward price is at the strike price.

- A call (put) option is OTM if the forward price is below (above) the strike price, i.e., the option has no intrinsic value.

To put it simply, OTM describes options which are unlikely to be exercised. ATM describes options where the strike is close to the forward rate for the tenor of the option and it is not clear whether such options will be exercised or not. ITM describes options which are more likely to be exercised.

For all spot values less than the strike the option is worthless and the holder has lost the premium. The payoff occurs once spot moves above the strike and the option has value. This is applicable to someone who is or will be short GBP and long USD, i.e., someone looking to reduce risk. Alternatively, it could be someone who believed GBP was going to appreciate against USD and wished to express this view via an option, i.e., they are taking a risk, limited to the premium, to try to make a profit. In these cases I am referring to option values at maturity.

Time value

The time value of an option (before expiry) represents the uncertainty in the value of the underlying currency pair at maturity. For the buyer of an option, this uncertainty is a good thing as it increases the probability that the option will end up in the money at maturity. For the seller of the option, the uncertainty is a bad thing as it means there is a greater likelihood of having to pay out at maturity. The degree of uncertainty in the final price of spot at option expiry increases (decreases) with a longer (shorter) time to maturity and a higher (lower) volatility in the price of the underlying currency pair.

The main components of time value are:

- days to maturity, i.e., time

- implied volatility

- the difference between the strike and the underlying foreign exchange rate, irrespective of whether it is ITM or OTM

- interest rates.

You can look at time value as a measure of how much the option may increase in value between now and the expiry date. This optionality is essentially due to volatility in the underlying asset. Even if the option is in the money it will have a time value which reflects the possibility that the option will have an even higher intrinsic value at expiry. The effect of time to expiry is similar to that of volatility – increasing time increases the price of the option.

When the option strike is at or close to the underlying forward exchange rate (ATM) the chance of the option moving to ITM status is considered to be 50:50. Therefore, the uncertainty of whether the option will be exercised on the expiry date is highest at this level (with relation to time value only, ignoring intrinsic value).

In the case of an OTM or ITM option the expectations are no longer 50:50 but are more certain. This results in lower time value, converging towards zero time value. At such a point the option premium would be either zero for an OTM option, or intrinsic value for an ITM option. This represents the fact that such options have effectively zero chance of being exercised (OTM), or zero chance of not being exercised (ITM).

It is important to remember that time value is not linear. Time value decays at an accelerating rate towards maturity, with little decay at the beginning of longer-term options. As a general rule of thumb, time value declines by one-third in the first half of the life of an option with the other two-thirds running off in the second half. This is illustrated in Figure 6.1.

Figure 6.1 – Time value decay as the expiry date of an option approaches

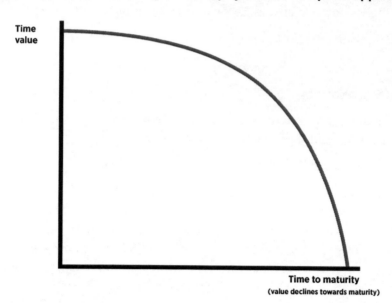

Time
value

Time to maturity
(value declines towards maturity)

Premium

The premium of an option (the price paid for the right to use the option) is essentially the sum of its intrinsic value and its time value. In other words, the premium is the present value of an option's expected payout. The premium is normally paid two business days after the trade date and may be quoted as a percentage of one of the underlying currencies or in foreign exchange pips.

Looking more closely, the premium is effectively determined by three factors:

- the *payout value* of the option (determined by the strike)

- the *probability* of the payout (determined by the volatility and the forward)

- the *discount factor* (determined by the time to maturity and interest rate).

In theory, the premium will equal the expected payout, which will also equal the expected cost of hedging the option. As the strike of a call increases, the expected payout of a call decreases, which in turn reduces the price.As the strike of a put increases, the expected payout of a put increases and, therefore, the price increases for a put.

Greater volatility in a currency pair increases the probability of an extreme price move and since the option premium partly depends on this probability, increasing volatility increases the premium of the option. As noted above, the effect of time to expiry is similar to volatility; increasing time increases the premium of the option. Figure 6.2 illustrates the profit and loss of an option.

Figure 6.2 – Profit and loss graph three months before expiration

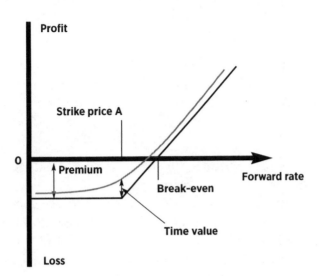

As Figure 6.2 shows, the value of the option with some time to expiry is always greater than the intrinsic value on the day of expiry. As noted above, the time value of an option is at a maximum when spot is close to the strike, i.e., when the uncertainty of whether the option is to be exercised is at a maximum.

Simple call and put options at expiry

With options it is very important to incorporate the premium paid or received (usually quoted as a percentage of the notional or in pips), and a profit and loss calculation, in assessing the value of the option and whether it should be implemented as a strategy. The following standard/vanilla call and put options are the basis for the construction of more complex strategies.

For example, let's look at a six-month GBP call/USD put trade made on 21 February 2010.

- Amount: GBP 2m
- Expiry: 19/8/10
- Maturity: 23/8/10
- Strike: 1.618

The premium is given as a percentage of the GBP trade amount and is 2.865%. Therefore, the premium is GBP 2,000,000 x 2.865% = GBP 57,300.

The equivalent USD pips quoted was 0.0465 and using this figure the premium would be GBP 2,000,000 x 0.0465 = USD 93,000. USD 93,000 in GBP = GBP 57,478.37 (USD 93,000/1.618).

The break-even point for this option will be 1.618 + 0.0465 = 1.6645. So if the spot for GBP/USD is above 1.6645 on the date of the option's expiry the option will be profitable and the option holder will exercise it.

Long call

The break-even rate for the buyer of a call will be equal to the strike price plus the premium paid for the option. This is easy to calculate if the premium is in pips. You expect the call currency to rise and therefore expect the put currency to fall. Implicitly, since the trader is long an option, they believe either that volatility will rise or at least that it will not fall. Volatility though can fall and the option buyer can still make money, as long as the spot moves in the right direction. There is unlimited profit potential and losses are limited to the premium paid. Figure 6.3 illustrates a long call option.

Figure 6.3 – Illustration of a long call option

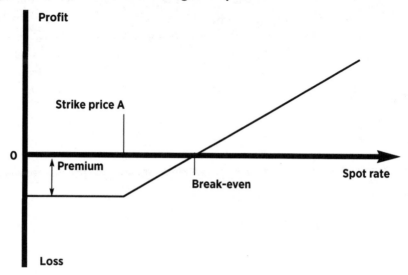

Short call

The break-even rate for the seller of a call will be equal to the strike price plus the premium received for the option. There is unlimited loss potential and profit is limited to the premium received. The seller gives the right to the buyer to buy the underlying currency at the strike price. This is a bearish strategy which generates immediate income. Since the seller is short an option, the seller believes either that volatility will fall or at least will not rise. Volatility though can rise and the option buyer can still make money, as long as the spot moves in the right direction. Figure 6.4 illustrates a short call option.

Figure 6.4 – Illustration of a short call option

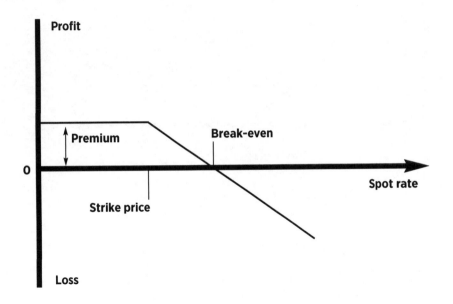

Long put

The break-even rate for the buyer of a put will be equal to the strike price minus the premium paid for the option. This option gives the buyer the right to sell the underlying currency at the strike price. The maximum loss is the initial premium. The buyer is expressing a bearish view of the underlying currency. Since they are long of an option they also implicitly believe either that volatility will rise or at least not fall. Figure 6.5 illustrates a long put option.

Figure 6.5 – Illustration of a long put option

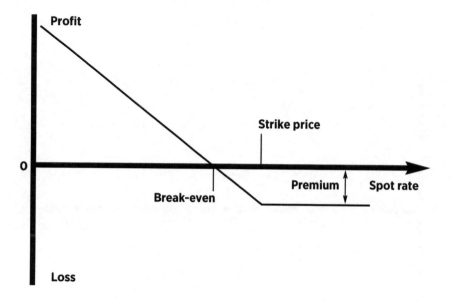

Short put

The break-even rate for the seller of a put will be equal to the strike price minus the premium received for the option. The seller gives the right to the buyer to sell the underlying currency at the strike price. The fundamental view of this strategy is that the put seller believes that underlying will not go down very much. This is a bullish strategy which generates immediate income. Since the seller is short an option they believe that either volatility will fall, or at least that it will not rise. Loss can be greater than the initial premium. Figure 6.6 illustrates a short put option.

Figure 6.6 – Illustration of a short put option

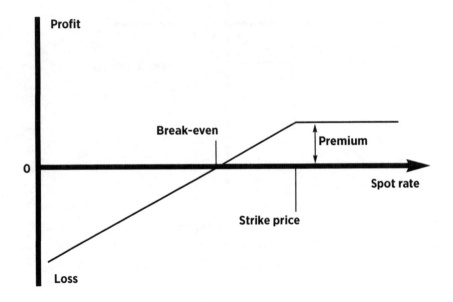

Combining options to create a synthetic forward put/call parity

Figure 6.7 – Illustration of a synthetic forward put/call option

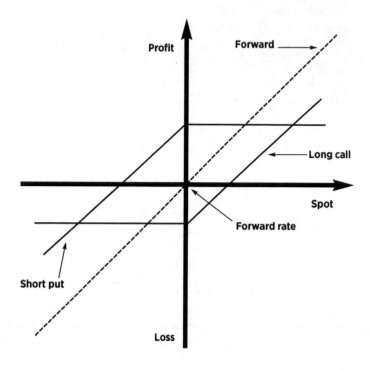

A forward purchase of a currency represents the purchase of a call and the sale of a put struck at the forward rate. A put and call struck at the forward rate are of equal value. The forward rate is the only strike at which both puts and calls have zero intrinsic value.

- Long forward = long call + short put

- Short forward = short call + long put

The Greeks

The relationship between the price of an option and its inputs are called 'Greeks', after various letters of the Greek alphabet. For some users it is very important to know how much the value of an option will change for a given change in market parameters, e.g., time, volatility, etc.

This information is generally for those who are seeking to dynamically manage the risk of an option over time, such as traders or funds. Many users of options may be unconcerned as to how the counterparty hedges and so will only have a passing interest in this section.

The Greeks are:

1. *Delta*: the sensitivity of the price to spot. This indicates the probability that the option will be exercised and how much spot to hold as the delta hedge.

2. *Gamma*: the sensitivity of delta to spot. This shows how quickly the delta changes for a change in spot.

3. *Vega*: the sensitivity of the option price to volatility.

4. *Theta*: the sensitivity of the option price to time. This shows how much the option will make or lose from one day to the next.

5. *Rho*: the sensitivity of the option value with respect to a change in the risk-free interest rate

We will now look at these in turn.

1. Delta (hedge ratio)

Delta is usually defined as the rate of change of the option's premium relative to a change in the underlying spot rate, i.e., the sensitivity of the price of an option to a change in spot. The delta of an option can have a value between -1 and 1 but is usually expressed in percentage terms. Options which are very OTM are described as low delta options while options which are very ITM are called high delta options.

The delta of an option approximately represents the probability of the option being exercised, i.e., of the option being ITM. Another way to look at the delta is that it tells you how closely the option behaves like a forward.

Delta changes during the life of the option. It is never static. If the spot or forward rate changes then the delta will change as the probability of exercise will have changed.

Example: an option to sell GBP 5m at 1.65 (GBP/USD)

When the spot is at 1.5 the option is deep ITM. It is more or less guaranteed to be exercised and in effect this option represents a forward to sell GBP 5m; therefore, delta in this case is GBP 5m, or 100%.

When the spot is at 1.95 the option is very OTM. There is very little chance of exercise and the option is more or less worthless. The worth of the option will be virtually unchanged for quite a range of spot values, hence the delta is zero. When the spot is close to the strike, i.e., 1.65, this option is ATM. The delta in this case will be 50% – the probability of the option being exercised is roughly 50/50.

Traders will often refer to an option by its delta. A '50 delta GBP call' is an ATM option which has a 50% chance of being in the money at expiry. A '25 delta GBP call' is an out OTM option which has just a 25% chance of being ITM at expiry. Delta is lower for OTM options and higher for ITM options.

Delta hedge

Delta hedging takes spot risk out of the option. The trader then has a position in volatility, time and interest rates. With a volatility trade the trader is not taking a view as to whether the spot rate will rise or fall but rather a view on the volatility of the currency pair.

When the option desk trades an option, the delta hedge for the option is usually executed. The new option position might be closing an opposite delta position, which balances the books without putting on a spot trade. In many cases the hedge is traded directly in the spot market rather than with the customer, as the customer is often transacting the option to hedge their underlying exposure.

If a trader has bought a GBP call/USD put then they will make money on a higher spot. Therefore, to construct an option and hedge combination whose total value remains constant for a rise in spot, the dealer has to sell spot against the option. The delta of the option tells the dealer exactly how much spot to sell.

Then, if the spot rate moves, the change in value of the option and of the forward trade will cancel each other out. In practice, because the delta changes as the spot rate changes, the size of this forward deal will need to be adjusted regularly and therefore the options trader will usually keep the delta for spot value. The trader is thus executing a position in the underlying foreign exchange market to hedge an option against any potential exercise.

Figure 6.8 shows a delta hedge. The lines show the payoff of the option, the hedge which makes money on a lower spot and the value of the combined option and hedge. The payoff is flat at the current spot rate of 1.65.

Figure 6.8 – A delta hedge

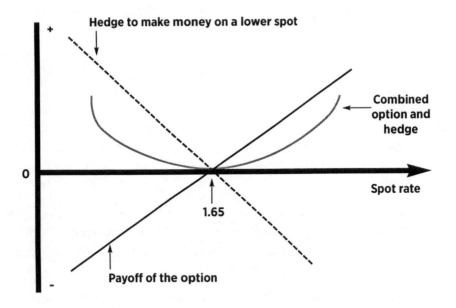

Examples of the delta hedge

- USD/JPY spot is 85 and a customer has bought USD 100m of a three-month 90 call (a delta of 15%), with no hedge. The bank will have to do a trade in the spot market to delta hedge this. The amount of the trade is 15% of the face amount (15% of USD 100m), so USD 15m. The option is a USD call so as spot goes up the option increases in worth and as the bank has sold it will lose money. Hence, the hedge is to buy spot. All option trades are made delta neutral at the point of trade. The spot will almost certainly move throughout the life of the option and further hedges will be required.

- GBP/USD spot is 1.65 and the bank has bought GBP 10m of a one-month 1.65 put (a delta of 50%) with no hedge. The option is a GBP put so it will make money on a lower spot. The hedge is 50% of GBP 10m, i.e., GBP 5m. The bank has bought the option so the bank will make a profit on a lower spot and hence should buy GBP 5m spot as the hedge. If a rise in GBP/USD to 1.67 changes the delta to 0.6, then the writer must purchase another GBP 1m to remain delta neutral.

- A customer sells GBP 10m of a one-year, 1.70 GBP put/USD call with spot at 1.79. The delta is 25. Hence, a delta hedge is to buy 25% of the face amount, which is GBP 2.5m (25% of GBP 10m).

2. Gamma

Gamma is a measure of the sensitivity of delta to a change in spot and is a useful tool in calculating risk within an option portfolio. Gamma therefore shows the option delta's sensitivity to market price changes. Gamma increases as the option moves from being in-the-money reaching its peak when the option is at-the-money. As the option moves out-of-the-money the gamma then decreases.

One way to visualise delta and gamma is to compare option pricing with driving a car on the motorway. If the car's position is considered the option price then the car's speed is the delta and the change in speed of the car (acceleration/deceleration) is gamma.

The gamma value is the same for puts of similar expiration and 'moneyness'. If you are long a call or a put, the gamma will be a positive number. If you are short a call or a put, the gamma will be a negative number.

The nearer the strike to the underlying foreign exchange rate, the higher the gamma. It will be at a maximum for ATM options. The higher the gamma the quicker the delta changes for a given change in spot and the quicker that the option moves in or out of the money.

When spot is a long way from the strike the gamma approaches zero reflecting the fact that at these spot levels the delta is pretty much constant (either 0 or 100) and is independent of spot.

The amount of gamma that an option has is also a function of time to expiry. The gamma increases as the time to expiry falls. Short-dated options have the biggest maximum gamma. This shows that short-dated options move more quickly from deep OTM to deep ITM than long-dated options. Intuitively one can see that the possible range of spot values on the expiry date in six months' time is very large compared to say a one-week option, where a relatively small movement in spot can shift the delta from around 50 to almost 100.

3. Vega

Vega is the sensitivity of the option price to a change in volatility. For all options an increase in volatility represents an increase in premium. Like gamma, if you are long options the vega is always positive and is at a maximum for ATM options if you are short options. Vega increases as the term increases at all levels of spot. Vega is proportional to the square root of the time to expiry.

4. Theta

Theta is also called 'time decay' and tells you how the value of the option changes as the time to expiry changes. It is normally quoted as the difference in the value of the option today and the value tomorrow. It will therefore show how much the option will make or lose from one day to the next, assuming all other parameters remain unchanged. Theta is greatest for ATM options and is much greater for short-dated options than long-dated options.

5. Rho

Rho tends to be of minor importance as interest rates are normally stable. Except under extreme circumstances, the value of an option is less sensitive to changes in the risk-free interest rate than to changes in other parameters such as Delta and Gamma. For this reason, rho is the least used of the first-order Greeks.

Rho is typically expressed as the amount of money the value of the option will gain or lose as the risk free interest rate rises or falls by 1% per annum (100 basis points).

Volatility (vol)

Volatility is a measure of the degree of variation in the price of the underlying currency rate. It is the key component of an option's time value and so the price of the option. Formally, it is defined as the standard deviation of the price changes over periodic intervals (i.e. daily, weekly, monthly) and comes in at least two basic forms: historical and implied. Historical volatility is the volatility as measured by using past price history for the relevant currency pair. It is highly dependent on the period used to estimate it as the true volatility of most financial assets changes over time and the historical measure is basically an average. Implied volatility is a measure of market expectations for future volatility and is directly related to option prices: given one you can automatically calculate the other. This is so much so that option prices are sometimes quoted in terms of implied volatility.

Models such as Black–Scholes calculate the theoretical fair price of an option. Using the model, the premium cost will imply a certain level of volatility. Implied volatilities are actually derived from trading and are therefore prices which can be adjusted by market makers to fit their own requirements.

A difference between implied volatility and historical volatility suggests that the market believes that future performance will be different from the past. The 'vol' that is used for the pricing of any option is constantly changing. This is driven by how volatile spot has been and expectations of future moves based on economic and political events.

As we have seen, the price of an option is directly related to the spot price. If an option is held as part of a delta neutral portfolio, movements in the spot price will be hedged out, and then the next most important factor in determining the value of the option will be its implied volatility. Increasingly banks and hedge funds are looking to trade volatility.

Given the importance of volatility to option pricing it is remarkable how infrequently it is mentioned, apart from within the professional market.

Impact of volatility on the Greeks

In the case of ATM options, when volatility goes up a given change in spot will have less of a bearing on the probability of the option being exercised; hence the delta is less sensitive to the spot move and the gamma is lower.

For low delta options the probability of the option being exercised is low and is insensitive to a move in spot. A rise in volatility in this situation can increase the probability of exercise, in which case the delta becomes more sensitive to a spot move and the gamma is higher. In the case of OTM options, when the volatility rises all OTM options move closer to being ATM. As ATM options have more volatility than OTM options both vega and theta will increase.

Volatility and pricing

The basis of the modern option pricing theory was the work of Fisher Black and Myron Scholes in the early 1970s. They attempted to produce a fair value for options on equities. Of course, foreign exchange options differ because there is no dividend and both currencies of the exchanges carry interest rates that can be fixed until maturity. Hence various adaptations have been made to the original Black–Scholes formula. It is not necessary to know the exact Black–Scholes formula or how it is derived, but it is more important to know what the inputs are and how the inputs affect the price.

The Black–Scholes pricing model assumes that the volatility of spot will be continuous over the lifetime of an option. This results in prices which are too low for extreme high and low strikes. The markets will price OTM options using higher implied vols because they know that market returns are not normally distributed. The pricing of options using a higher volatility for strikes that are a long way from spot creates a volatility smile (see Figure 6.9).

Figure 6.9 – The volatility smile

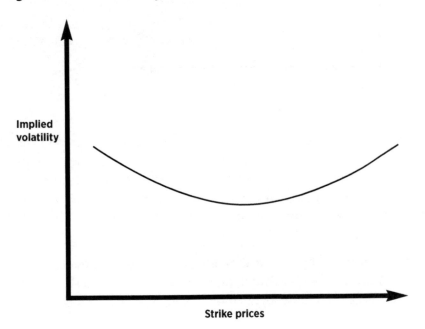

The volatility smile shows that implied volatility is higher as the options go more ITM and OTM. The smile is most evident in short-dated speculative options; there is bigger option trading demand for ITM and OTM options than ATM options.

There is often a skew to the volatility smile, called the 'risk reversal' (see Figure 6.10).

Figure 6.10 – The volatility skew

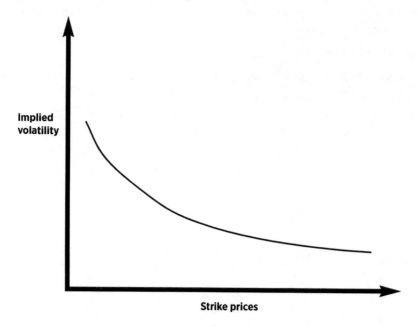

This volatility skew is particularly evident in currency pairs where there is a large interest rate differential between the currencies, or where there is a large difference in the expected volatility of spot for an up move compared to a down move (in emerging market currencies, for example and when the government is intervening to protect the currency or runs a potentially breachable peg).

The smile shape is usually generated by using three commonly traded strikes. These are the ATM, the 25 delta put and the 25 delta call. The shape of the smile alters depending on supply and demand, how spot is moving, and market expectations.

Volatility is constantly changing on expectations of future economic and political events and therefore so is the pricing. The volatility for a one-month ATM option is likely to be different from that for a one-year ATM option. With a short-term bout of volatility the price of a one-month option will rise to reflect this short-term uncertainty. The one-year options will not be affected by this to the same extent.

How options are priced

To recap, the following factors are required to price an option:

1. Call or put

2. Currency pair

3. Strike rate

4. Amount

5. Style (European, American or Asian)

6. Expiration date and time

7. Spot foreign exchange rate

8. Interest rates for each currency

9. Implied volatility of the currency pair

Factors 1-6 are chosen. Factors 7-8 are taken from their respective markets. The last factor (9) is peculiar to options and represents the anticipated volatility of the currency pair over the life of the option and is the only unknown factor in the option price.

Professional traders will make prices in volatility since the premium is easily calculated once this has been agreed. Volatility, expressed as the annualised percentage rate of change of a currency pair, is the key component of an option's time value and therefore also in the price of the option. High volatility equals high premium; low volatility results in low premium.

Option prices are quoted by dealers in these three main ways:

• Volatility for a given delta: In this case you would then have to calculate the price from the model.

• Percentage of the face value amount: Taking a GBP call/USD put in GBP 2,000,000, if the price is a percentage of GBP at 2.4%, the premium is 2,000,000 x 2.4% = GBP 48,000.

• Pips of the face amount: Taking a GBP call/USD put in GBP 2,000,000, if the price in pips is 190 then the premium is GBP 2,000,000 x 0.019 = GBP 38,000.

Making an option transaction

If you are buying an option you will need to tell the bank the following:

1. Call or put on which currencies.

2. Expiry and value dates.

3. Strike rate and/or the delta.

4. Amount.

5. How you want the price quoted.

6. For indicative quotes (i.e., rates which are not binding), what spot rate you want the indication based off.

7. You must also decide if you want to delta hedge the position. If you do not trade the delta then the option can be a hedge against a foreign exchange position. If you delta hedge you remove the spot risk from the option and it will not then be a hedge against a foreign exchange position – it will be a trading position in volatility and time. If you do make a spot delta trade you will do this with the bank you trade the option with. You will usually tell the bank the strike and the delta of the option and ask for the volatility. You would in these circumstances be expected to have an option pricing system and be able to price the option from the volatility quote.

Basic option strategies

Bull (call) spread

A bullish view is expecting the price to rise. The bull (call) spread strategy can be created by buying a call option (paying a premium) with a certain strike price and selling a call option (receiving a premium) with a higher strike price (such that the ratio of their notionals is 1:1). This enables the cost to be reduced at the expense of limiting the participation in the appreciation of the underlying currency to the strike rate of the sold option.

Take a three-month trade with spot GBP/USD 1.625. A bull spread may look as shown in Figure 6.11 if the topside is viewed around 1.65.

Figure 6.11 – The bull (call) spread

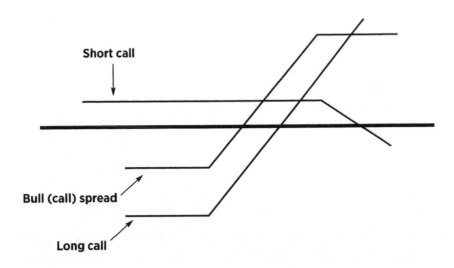

In this example the notional amount is GBP 1m. The trader buys a GBP call/USD put strike 1.625 and sells a GBP call/USD put 1.65. The transaction date is 3/3/11, expiry is 3/6/11 and delivery is 7/6/11 (weekend 4/5 June) for both options. The cost of the buy call is GBP 18,150 (1.815% of GBP) and the receipt from the sell call is GBP 11,600 (1.16% of GBP), a difference of GBP 6,550 payable. This represents the maximum potential loss from the trade. This is equivalent to GBP/USD pips 0.0106, which means that a GBP/USD rate of 1.6356 is required to break-even. The sale of the call puts a limit on any potential gain to 1.65.

This is cheaper than a vanilla option for a bullish view on the underlying currency but with a limited view to the upside. This is a conservative strategy with loss limited to the cost of the net premium paid. An equivalent position is to buy the lower strike put and sell the higher strike put.

If a trader believes that the spot will go down but the move will be limited they could buy a put spread. In this case they would sell a low strike put (receive premium) and buy a high strike put (pay premium). Again the maximum loss is the net premium paid.

Collar, risk reversal, range forward

Figure 6.12 – Collar, risk reversal, range forward

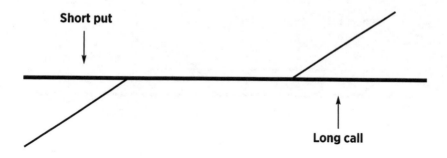

A collar, risk reversal, range forward strategy is comprised of a long call position (bought an option) combined with a short put position (sold as an option), as shown in Figure 6.12. The strikes on the call and put are normally chosen such that the strategy is zero cost. You will see an actual example of this at the end of this chapter where we look at options in practice. A risk reversal also refers to buying a put and selling a call.

This is a mildly bullish strategy that has appeal because of the low cost and is less risky than taking a forward outright position. As we have seen, if the strike of the call and the put are the same then the net exposure is the same as a forward in the underlying currencies, i.e., the optionality is removed. In the zero cost format it does severely limit upside gains.

Long straddle

Figure 6.13 – Long straddle

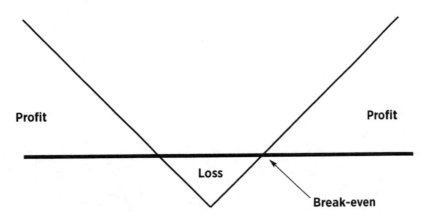

The long straddle strategy is created by purchasing both a call and put option on the underlying currency with the same strike and time to expiry, as illustrated in Figure 6.13. This is normally used as a speculative instrument where movement of the underlying spot is expected but the direction is uncertain. This is a strategy for buying volatility as the initial delta (sensitivity to spot) is close to zero. The cost is high (two premiums) so a large movement in spot or volatility is required to make money. Profit potential is unlimited in either direction but loss is limited to the premium paid.

The straddle is often sold to generate premium income when spot is seen to be range bound. This is a strategy for going short implied volatility.

Strangle

Figure 6.14 – Strangle

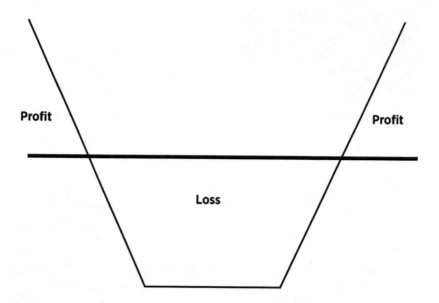

The strangle is a variation of the straddle. It is illustrated in Figure 6.14. The strangle is normally used as a speculative instrument. Again, movement of the underlying exchange rate is expected but direction is uncertain. The cost is high with two premiums but lower than that of the straddle due to the two strikes being OTM, but this, however, sets the break-even points further away. Hence a very strong movement is required in the spot in order to reach the profit regions.

Covered call or dual currency strategy

Taking an example of GBP/USD, this strategy offers the opportunity to significantly enhance the yield of a standard deposit rate by placing the funds in an investment that will be repaid in either sterling or dollars, depending upon the movement of the exchange rate. It is usually assumed that the customer is indifferent to holding either sterling or dollars. This strategy is usually sold with the option embedded in the product. This can be quite restricting, but of course the option could be executed independently.

The customer will be shown a yield set against a desired strike rate. The additional yield is generated from the sale of a GBP call/USD put, for which the customer receives a premium. By writing the call option the customer has put a cap on the upside relative to the put currency. Banks usually offer this product with amounts ranging from a surprisingly low GBP 25,000 up into the millions. There must be an option market in the currencies with a high degree of liquidity. Maturities are normally two weeks to one month, but longer periods can be chosen.

The covered call strategy is not suitable for customers who have a requirement for, say, dollars in the relatively short term. A spot or a forward transaction will provide more certainty in this situation. The risk in this case is that GBP/USD could fall during the life of the structure and then, at expiry, if the reference rate fixes below the strike price, the principal and accrued interest will be repaid in sterling.

If the reference price is at or above the strike price at maturity the principal and accrued interest will be converted into dollars at the strike price. Market movements in the exchange rate before and after expiry date are not of consequence.

I view this as a yield-enhancing strategy where the investor has sufficient funds to be flexible in their currency allocation. While it is normally assumed that the customer is indifferent to what currency they may hold, from my experience no one is indifferent to the price they have bought or sold at. Clearly if they need to convert the alternative currency back into the original currency there is a risk of loss.

Example of a covered call option

Table 6.23 – Summary of terms for a dual currency deposit (covered call option)

Currency pair	GBP/USD
Principal amount	GBP 1m
Trade date	23 November 2009
Value date	25 November 2009
Determination/Expiry date	29 December 2009
Maturity date (two working days)	31 December 2009
Interest rate	5% p.a. (5.11% AER)
Spot price	1.6616
Strike price	1.6970
Reference rate	GBP/USD spot exchange rate at 10 am New York time for the US and European time zones and 2 pm Singapore time for the Asian time zones.
Repayment amount (including interest)	(1) If the reference price on the determination date fixes below the strike price: GBP 1,004, 931.51. Interest is always paid in the principal currency. (2) If the reference price on the determination date fixes at or above the strike price: USD 1,705,368.77 (GBP 1,004,931.51 x 1.6970).
Day count	Actual/365
Delivery	Sterling or US dollar
Fees	% p.a. of the principal amount
Calculation agent	Big bank

This covered call option is illustrated in Figure 6.15.

Figure 6.15 – Redemption profile of a covered call option

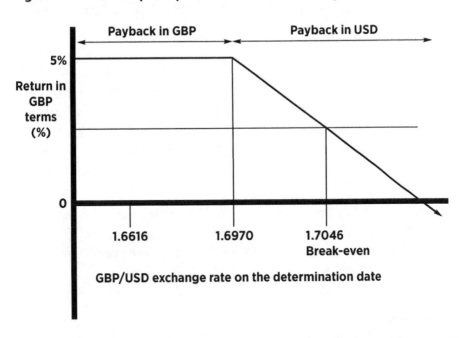

The structure outlined here will repay a fixed amount of either sterling or US dollars on the maturity date. Enhanced interest of 5% p.a. (5.11% AER) will also be paid on the maturity date in sterling or the equivalent amount converted into US dollars if the exchange rate fixes at or above the strike price on the determination date. In our example the deposit principal is also guaranteed either in sterling if no conversion takes place, or US dollars if the conversion takes place.

These structures are attractive in a low interest environment, when there is a lack of investment opportunities and when foreign exchange volatility is high. The higher the volatility, the higher the premium received, and the higher the enhanced return. These may also be attractive to customers with regular flows in different currency pairs or those who need to convert cash from one currency to another but with no immediate need to do so.

These structures should not be used for foreign exchange trading, or with a view to execute a single transaction for a known requirement at a specified date in the future. It would be better to write your own options, not least because of the fees involved with these covered call structures.

Writing options for yourself is really a professional alternative and requires a fair degree of option knowledge and access to pricing platforms. I think a good application of this type of structure is within a large multi-currency cash fund. Currency weightings can be adjusted at the margin while increasing returns.

Exotic options

The currency option is a derivative of the foreign exchange market. More advanced options – 'exotic options', as they are regularly referred to – are derivatives of the ordinary or plain vanilla options described above. These options have been developed by banks and tailored to specific client needs, either to better match the risk profile of the customer or simply to reduce premium expenditure.

The latter point has been a key factor for UK corporates, who have been reluctant to pay premiums. It is important to remember, however, that if you pay less for an option then almost certainly some of the benefits have been reduced.

Barrier options

A barrier option is a conventional option except that it is changed in a predetermined way when the underlying trades at a predetermined barrier level. Barrier options are therefore path dependent and consist of two types: *knock-in* and *knock-out*.

A knock-in option pays nothing at expiry unless at some point in its life the underlying reaches a pre-set barrier and brings the option to life as a standard call or put. A knock-out option is a conventional option until the price of the underlying reaches a pre-set barrier price, in which case it is extinguished and ceases to exist. Barrier options have both a strike price and a barrier price which may be made active for part or all of the option's life. Both types of barriers can be set ITM or OTM.

Digital/binary

A digital/binary option pays out a fixed amount if the underlying satisfies a pre-determined trigger level, or else pays nothing. At maturity, European forms of this option pay out only if the spot rate trades above (or below) the trigger level at expiry. With American forms, pay out occurs if the spot rate trades through the trigger level at any time up to and including expiry (this is a one-touch situation – if the spot rate touches the trigger level once, at any time, the pay out occurs). If spot fails to achieve the trigger level during the life of the option then the option pays nothing.

I have mentioned these advanced options because market commentaries will regularly refer to them. In some cases, enormous payouts are at stake and there have been reports of banks buying or selling to protect levels being triggered. On some occasions protection is successful and on others it is not. When it is not, the price action can be quite violent as the bank that was buying/selling to protect the position is forced to unwind.

Options in practice

1. Hedging a contingent exposure

ABC Plc is a UK company which manufactures and installs hospital operating theatres. It is bidding for a contract to supply three theatres for a new military hospital in California in the US. It is in competition with two other companies and has been asked to quote in US dollars, which will be the paying currency.

ABC has budgeted the cost to manufacture and install at GBP 20m. ABC Plc plan to bid at USD 40m, which represents receipt of GBP 25m given the current exchange rate of 1.6. The US Government allow a six-month review process on the respective bids and therefore ABC is exposed to movements in GBP/USD. There are several ways that ABC Plc can deal with this potential foreign exchange exposure:

- Do nothing, wait to see if they win the contract and then sell USD 40m for sterling.

- Sell dollars and buy sterling six-months forward.

- Buy a six-month sterling call/dollar put option.

If ABC waits for six months it is subject to foreign exchange risk. If sterling appreciates to, say, 1.7, it will only receive GBP 23.53m for the contracted USD 40m, thus materially eroding its profit margin. Clearly, if sterling depreciates it will make an even greater profit.

Let's say that ABC executes a *six-month forward contract* where it sells USD 40m for sterling. There is an obligation to settle this contract whatever the outcome of the bid. Therefore, if they are unsuccessful they will be left with a short dollar, long sterling exposure in six months' time. If sterling, for example, appreciates to 1.75 then ABC can make a profit: if below 1.6 they will close out the position at a loss. Apart from this major drawback, a forward contract, unlike an option, will not allow participation in a depreciation of sterling.

Looking at some example figures for the six-month forward contract:

ABC sells USD 40m at 1.6 = GBP 25m. ABC closes out position:

If the GBP/USD exchange rate is 1.75 in sixth months time ABC buys USD 40m and sells GBP 22,857,142: a profit of GBP 2,142,858 (GBP 25,000,000 - GBP 22,857,142).

If the GBP/USD rate is 1.55 ABC buys USD 40m and sells GBP 25,806,451: a loss of GBP 806,451 (GBP 25,806,451 - GBP 25,000,000).

Alternatively, if ABC purchases a *sterling call* it has a guaranteed maximum exchange rate but can still benefit if sterling depreciates in the next six months. If ABC fails to win the contract its loss will be limited to the price of the option. There is of course potential for a profit on the option.

Of the three alternatives, the option is the best for a risk-averse company. ABC buys a six-month dollar put, sterling call on USD 40m, at a strike of 1.6. If ABC wins the contract and if the exchange rate rises above 1.6, ABC will exercise the option at 1.6. If the exchange rate is below 1.6, ABC will not exercise the option and will deal in the spot market instead.

If ABC does not win the contract the option either expires worthless if the exchange rate is below 1.6, or can be traded at a profit if above.

2. Hedging a known exposure

XYZ Plc is a UK company and receives USD 3m a quarter from a service contract agreement. The policy of the company is to hedge all currency exposures when identified. The company will sell USD 3m for sterling at three-monthly intervals. The question here is not whether to do anything to reduce the currency exposure – the company policy is that they will always do this – but which method to use.

Unlike the first example above, here the amount and timing of the receipt of funds is known. The issue for the company is where to pitch the strike, which in turn determines the cost.

The company has three choices:

1. A USD put/GBP call.

2. A zero cost collar.

3. A plain forward contract.

The first point we can see from Table 6.24 is that the higher the strike, the cheaper the option premium. Second, it is important to note the break-even levels. Options carry a premium cost and the user needs to achieve a balance between the cost of purchasing the option and protection against currency exposure. Most users of options would not be looking to make the maximum profit on any upside, especially as it will involve extra cost; the primary goal for companies will be to protect their profit margin, albeit with some element of upside profit potential.

Therefore, zero cost options are an attractive alternative, as shown in Table 6.25. These will protect the downside, which in this example was set at 1.5, but will also limit any potential upside gains.

The plain forward contract is also worth considering. Here dollars will be sold at an agreed rate for the dates in question, which in all cases was under 1.43 (see Table 6.26). Inevitably, views on the current and forecast level of sterling will be integral to the decision.

In this case spot around 1.5 was considered good value, although there was no compelling reason to look for any material appreciation in sterling. The pricing alternatives are shown in the tables below and illustrate in practice how time and strike can impact the premium cost.

The client decides to cover half the exposure in the straight vanilla dollar put option and the remainder via forward contracts. The client chose to buy USD put/GBP call with strike 1.45 in USD 1.5m for 3m, 6m, 9m and 12m. This gave the client unlimited upside potential, albeit the cost of the longer-dated options did impact on the break-even level.

The client sells USD 1.5m for GBP every quarter at an outright rate below 1.43. With this arrangement, exposure has been hedged at good levels and some upside participation has been retained. The client will have a worst case average which, for example, in Q1 will be 1.4642 ((1.5042+1.4242)/2). Note I have calculated it using the break-even price. While the zero cost option did provide a worst case of 1.5 (and so a higher worst case than this average for Q1) the upside potential was limited.

Table 6.24 – Strike strategy: three different rates for USD put/GBP call, spot reference price 1.4244

	Strike/Break-even	Strike/Break-even	Strike/Break-even
3m	1.45/1.5042	1.50/1.5359	1.55/1.5740
Premium % USD	3.74	2.39	1.55
6m	1.45/1.5257	1.50/1.555	1.55/1.5909
Premium % USD	5.22	3.7	2.64
9m	1.45/1.5414	1.50/1.5706	1.55/1.6046
Premium % USD	6.3	4.71	3.52
12m	1.45/1.554	1.50/1.583	1.55/1.6159
Premium % USD	7.17	5.53	4.25

Table 6.25 – Zero cost collar strategy

Date	Cap	Collar
3 months	1.5	1.3575
6 months	1.5	1.37
9 months	1.5	1.385
12 months	1.5	1.4

Table 6.26 – Forward contract strategy

Date	Rate
3 months	1.4242
6 months	1.4246
9 months	1.425
12 months	1.4261

Options summary

When to use options

- For speculation on volatility, or for straight directional trades.

- For hedging, the premium payable means that currency options are expensive in comparison with using the foreign exchange forward market. To benefit from the particular advantages of currency options they should ideally be used when at least one of the following applies:

  - There is uncertainty about the amount and/or timing of currency exposures.

  - The customer making the hedge needs to establish a maximum cost of conversion but also wishes to benefit from any favourable movements in the exchange rate.

  - The customer wants to enhance the yield on their cash and is willing to take on spot risk.

Advantages

- Profit potential is unlimited on a long option.

- Loss is limited to the premium on a long option.

- Selling options provides income but doing this on its own is not advisable (i.e. an *uncovered* position – or not owning the underlying currency for delivery – is not a good strategy).

- Selling and buying options together can hedge the desired range at lower cost.

- Hedgers can lock in a minimum conversion value for their currency but also benefit from some or all of any favourable movements in the spot exchange rate (depending on the type of option).

- There is considerable flexibility regarding strike rate and maturity date, which in turn can provide a degree of flexibility in cost.

- Options can be used to hedge or trade currency volatility.

- Option activity can provide clues as to general future direction in the currency market.

Disadvantages

- Loss potential is unlimited in a short option.

- Gains are limited in a short option position.

- An outright option purchase involves the payment of a premium. When markets are volatile this can be prohibitively expensive.

- A reduction in premium cost is always allied to a reduction in any benefits from a favourable movement in the exchange rate.

- Liquidity in longer-dated maturities or in more exotic currency pairs is not as deep as in the forward foreign exchange market.

7.

PREDICTING THE FUTURE: TECHNICAL ANALYSIS AND FX FORECASTING

TECHNICAL ANALYSIS AND THE FOREIGN EXCHANGE MARKETS

Technical analysis is the study of price movements, primarily through charts, for the purpose of forecasting future price movements. Its predictive qualities are based on three premises:

1. The price contains all known information.

2. Prices move in trends.

3. History repeats itself.

Technical analysis has been around for many years but the rapid advances and availability of computer power have been responsible for growth in popularity of the approach in recent years. The ability to collect and retrieve vast amounts of data has been crucial to transforming this once fringe activity to mainstream participation.

The notion of cycles goes back to the Greeks. It is derived from the Greek word *Kuklos*, which means 'circle'. A cycle is a recurring interval of time within which a round of regularly repeated events is completed. It is undoubtedly the case that financial markets do seem to repeat the same cycles and the same patterns of events. However, while this may apply to the macro level, it is on the micro level that its effectiveness comes into question.

In favour of technical analysis

The main argument in favour of technical analysis is that there is more in a price than just numerical data – there are human emotions. By looking at the price action it helps you understand the nature of human behaviour; fear, greed and hope, and more importantly how these bear weight at any particular time.

Proponents of technical analysis cite a number of other supporting reasons. They say that it helps identify trends and where price action is in relation to those trends. It should be remembered that there is no current/live volume data available in the foreign exchange market; all data is historical. Technical analysis thus helps to track the demand/supply situation, and can be used to identify stop losses and price targets (take profits). It also enables the analyst to cover many markets in a short space of time without necessarily being an expert. There is, however, no method or indicator that will definitely provide consistent results.

Flaws of technical analysis

The biggest danger in using chart techniques is ourselves. Rather than looking for direction all we really want is confirmation and are prepared to choose a chart or indicator which suits our particular bias at the time. For some, technical analysis is used as a counter-argument to economists and the irrationality of human emotion in the market, and for others it is used in conjunction with a fundamental view.

Further, technical analysis is an attempt to *forecast* where financial markets are heading, and thus by its nature it is a prediction and not an exact science. The difference between technical analysis and other types of forecasting – such as weather forecasts – is that no one can change or even influence the weather, whereas a technical call on market direction can attract sufficient trading interest to validate the prediction. Having said this, the idea that charts are self-fulfilling does not really stack up – there is scant evidence of chartists dominating the marketplace except for during brief moments.

It should never be assumed that charts provide definitive views. Charts are usually open to interpretation, especially as there are a number of charting methodologies, each with their own particular focus. Even then, when the technical view appears in print, it is regularly punctuated by conditional clauses and then concluded with a chapter and verse disclaimer. In the appendix I have included an introduction to technical analysis patterns that will give you a basic understanding of the area and terminology regularly quoted.

FORECASTING THE FOREIGN EXCHANGE MARKETS

Over the past 30 years the growth in economic forecasting has been spectacular. What was once the chief dealer and a few traders having a chat about the markets on a Friday afternoon, pronouncing the next 12 months' forecasts for GBP/USD, is now a large group of academic luminaries poring over models and data. The forecasts of these analysts are in huge demand, benefiting from cheap global communications and the insatiable desire of those in the markets to know the future.

At least at the outset technical analysts' and economists' methods are similar. They both use historical data to produce forecasts. The difference is that chartists look at market price action while economists look at economic data, make forecasts on this data and from this make an estimation of how a given currency will react.

The difficulty in currency forecasting is that you are always dealing with two currencies. It is also a dynamic process where deterministic models can fall short. The variants of purchasing power models will give a medium-term guide to an appropriate level, but will not help much in the shorter term, which in this context could be 12 months or more. A very good example of this was GBP/USD which reached the heady heights of 2 in the early 2000s despite fair value measures suggesting that the rate should be around 1.6; indeed, GBP/USD stayed up at around 2 for some time before the fall in price occurred.

There is a widely held view amongst economists (notably Keynes) that no one can make money in foreign exchange in the long run. This is essentially based on the view that currency forecasting is impossible. This then begs the question of whether we should trade short term or long term, or indeed if in practice, there is really any difference. Those who claim that they are in for the long term are not immune from short-term moves no matter how bizarre they are perceived to be. Risk management tools such as value at risk constraints, margin calls and stop loss orders are not term considerations; they are all priced from the current price. So even if you have a long-term goal it will be affected by short-term fluctuations. It is therefore very hard in these circumstances for a trader to stay with their initial trading goal.

In the opening chapter I described the various factors that can impact on exchange rates: interest rates, relative growth, debt, trade deficits and political events. This cocktail of causal factors is always present in the foreign exchange markets but we are never quite sure how to weight them or to weight their impact in time. In other words, it is difficult to judge how long it will be before a trade deficit matters, or debt or a political disturbance unnerves traders.

It is easy to be dismissive of these currency forecasters but just as is the case with chartists you cannot ignore them. They have a huge market profile and virtually instant visibility. A buy note for a currency issued by a forecaster can have the same short-term impact as that for a share.

8.

PSYCHOLOGY AND FOREIGN EXCHANGE

The book so far has been dominated by numbers. After all, any trade involves a buy and a sell which boils down to two numbers. However, the human psyche remains important. Indeed, for the trader, controlling emotions can be just as important as playing to a set of rules. I shall now discuss some psychological aspects that I believe to be key to trading.

GROUP BEHAVIOUR

The human condition is to work and live within groups. Humans feel more comfortable in groups, so there is a tendency to follow the current trend or the latest strategy. Underlying this is the desire not to be left behind. In this context we regularly read that analysts view a currency as extremely overvalued or, in plain language, they are saying the price is wrong. This happened to sterling in the 2000s. There was *eventually* a massive correction. As John Maynard Keynes described it, markets can stay wrong longer than you can stay solvent.

At the heart of buying any currency (or asset), whether it is perceived to be overvalued or not, is the belief that someone else will pay more for it later (often referred to as the *greater fool theory*). That being said, serious losses have been incurred trying to counter a market's irrational valuation.

It is not only our own judgements that will determine our final trading decision. We like to look to others for confirmation; the bigger the group the better. It was illuminating to read that some of the major hedge funds' leading lights gathered to discuss the euro in late 2009. They allegedly put on huge short positions afterwards. They were of course forced to unwind months later. In practice, traders are often concerned not just with what the average trader thinks but with what the average of the average traders' thoughts is.

OVERCONFIDENCE

A number of studies seem to prove the point that people tend to be overconfident in the reliability of their judgements.

Researchers have made studies where they ask participants to make a judgement on a large set of unrelated propositions. Examples are:

- How long is the Amazon River?

- What is the air distance from Paris to Sydney?

- How many bones are there in the human body?

Participants are asked to give minimum and maximum estimates. There are three possible outcomes – the real figure could be higher than the maximum estimate (this is a high surprise); the outcome could be lower than your lower estimate (a low surprise); or the outcome could be inside your confidence interval.

If you are a good judge of the limits of your knowledge you should expect to encounter approximately 1% high surprises and 1% low surprises, with the balance being within your confidence interval. However, a typical outcome in many studies is a surprise rate of 15-25%. This suggests that people set the confidence too tight or quite simply people have inflated ideas of their knowledge. If one is mindful of this natural bias, keeping a record of instances of one's overconfidence can help to frame trading decisions.

Optimism

Allied to overconfidence is optimism. Optimists will tend to underestimate the possibility of bad outcomes over which they have no control. They are also prone to illusions of control. They underestimate the role of chance and exaggerate the degree to which they control their fate or indeed events. While it is nice to keep a list of successes it is more useful to keep a list of failures and reasons for these.

Price action in the foreign exchange markets is always easy to explain the next day. You can hear it and you can read it from a whole range of commentators explaining with mathematical clarity why the market reacted as it did. This process, dealing backwards, leads us to conclude incorrectly that all indeed was predictable, which of course the price action contradicts.

While it is perfectly reasonable to rationalise the past, it has negative consequences. It not only fosters the illusion that the world is more predictable than it is, which promotes overconfidence, but it also makes a trade look reasonable one minute and incredibly rash the next.

OVERREACTION

A psychological trap prevalent in most markets is to overreact to chance events. The human condition is always looking for patterns and cycles to operate within. It works on the basis that an underlying factor is behind any notable sequence of events. This is of course the attraction of technical analysis. However, the danger is that people are too quick to see patterns where none actually exist. This does not just apply to foreign exchange – it applies to most fields of finance. The hedge fund or vocal economist can reap undue credibility for a limited run of success. This is sometimes called the *hot hand fallacy*, which is the tendency to attribute causal significance to chance fluctuations.

This was documented in a study of US basketball players.[8] The researchers tested the popular notion that players are sometimes hot and sometimes cold against the players' long-term average shooting success. The study failed to turn up more deviations from a player's long-term shooting percentage than one would expect to occur purely from chance.

The trading corollary is to ask yourself whether you know more than the market. This is probably a good question to ask before any trade. The other question to ask is whether the trade is based on random factors. In other words it is important to list your reasons for trading. If nothing else it will put a brake on overtrading instincts, largely prevalent in males.

ATTITUDE TO RISK

An important element of any trading is our attitude to risk or more specifically what weighting is given to losses versus gains. Let's say I offer you a bet on the toss of a coin. If you lose, you lose GBP 100. What is the minimal gain that would make this bet acceptable? The answer usually comes out around GBP 200 to GBP 250. This is a simple guide to your attitude to trading. This asymmetry is called 'loss aversion' but it is more often referred to as 'risk aversion'.

You could thus reasonably assume that the ideal foreign exchange trade would be one with much hope (possibility of gain) and little fear (possibility of loss).

---

[8] Gilovich, Vallone and Tversky (1985).

This should immediately suggest some option structure which limits the downside and offers some upside participation. However, an option usually comes with additional costs and, if not, then greatly reduced upside participation. As a result options are not generally favoured.

The successful trader should have a clear vision of their risk appetite at the outset. What was acceptable risk at the beginning of the trade may well change. Risk is dynamic across the asset classes and awareness of this is an essential ingredient for successful trading.

ATTITUDE TO RULES

Decision theorists start with the reasonable premise that trading decisions are made in situations of high complexity and high uncertainty, which rules out any reliance on fixed rules and forces the decision maker to rely on intuition. Intuitive trading, however, is prone to biases and illusions which lead to risk-taking that the trader is not aware of, and outcomes that were not anticipated. In other words, this is unwarranted trading. The skill is to recognise situations in which a particular error is likely and where intuition cannot be relied on; intuition must be supplemented by analytical or objective thinking, formulated into trading rules.

However, every generation or so declares that we are living in a new era. We therefore change the rules and rationalise our behaviour as being prudent and flexible. The foreign exchange markets are not exempt from this observation and with the proliferation of computers and electronic trading there is a danger that fundamental truths are ignored. I shall be discussing what I believe are the key elements to successful trading later but it is my view that trading rules are a constant over time.

The history we looked at in the opening chapter and the rise and fall of the carry trade are not merely academic asides; these examples from the past provide a platform to avoid trading follies in the future, or at least give you some guidance that might allow you see them in the making. The major failures in trading, investment or indeed government policy have occurred when the participants believe that the rules of nature, economics or the human psyche have somehow changed.

9.
INFLUENCES ON FOREIGN EXCHANGE MARKETS

As we have seen, understanding the foreign exchange markets requires not so much a grasp of economic history, fundamentals and theory as of the irrational way in which people can behave when they join together in crowds. However, it is still important to have an awareness of what influences the markets from a day-to-day perspective. In this chapter I will bring together and look at the various factors that influence the foreign exchange markets, starting with economic data.

ECONOMIC DATA

The economic data that influences the foreign exchange markets is by no means always the same data – influential data changes over the economic cycle and to some extent with economic fashion. In the early 1980s, with monetarists dominating policy, money supply figures were an important factor in determining exchange rates. In the 2007-09 crisis period central banks were the most influential factor with the US Federal Reserve announcements, notably in 2008, critical.

By 'influential', here I mean the ability to generate volatility in the market at the time of the announcement of the data. Ironically, although Bank of England Governor Mervyn King once said that the central banker's ambition was to be boring, his comments on sterling in 2009 and 2010 usually resulted in large sterling sales.

The US non-farm payrolls (employment figures) are very important data in determining the foreign exchange markets, although a major issue here is forecasting error. It should be noted that the US jobs data is usually released on a Friday afternoon, 1.30 pm London time. If this coincides with a week where there has been a large move in the market then there is scope for sharp position correction on the release. The impact of this data can be further exaggerated if the Friday is a month or quarter end, or if there is a public holiday on the Monday.

A further consideration is if there is a number of economic data releases on the same day which can pull in opposite directions. For example, in 2009 and

2010 US CPI data was prominent, with the inflation/deflation debate that was a major talking point at the time, but there is often industrial production and consumer sentiment released on the same day.

Trade figures are still very important but individual releases no longer have any real shock value. The cumulative effect of deficits, however,, will still weigh on a currency over time. The US trades were very influential in the early to mid 2000s as the deficit spiralled but have been less important of late as the deficit eased under a weakening dollar. The collapse in the US housing market in 2008 arguably triggered the downturn in the US economy and for a brief time housing data were the figures to watch.

European data does not really have the same potential impact on foreign exchange markets as the US data does. ECB announcements are by far the most influential.

The clear message here is that data impact changes over time so when observing the foreign exchange markets you should be aware of what news is considered important at that time.

While a foreign exchange position might be viewed as medium or long term, the trader will be regularly tested on an intra-day basis. As noted above, the key economic releases or central bank announcements are an obvious pressure point and these may force traders to reconsider positions or, indeed, the price movements may force them out via stop loss orders. In addition, there are various fixing times which have increased in importance as corporates and funds are obliged to trade at these specific times to achieve benchmark price levels.

The two most important fixing times are the ECB fix at 14.15 CET and the 16.00 fix, London time. In practice, these fixing times merely tend to concentrate volatility around these particular times as the big trading banks endeavour to fill their customer orders. This becomes even more acute on month end and quarter end when funds are required to rebalance their currency exposure in their portfolios against a benchmark rate.

International fund managers have an incentive to follow the hedging practice of their benchmark indices, and the change in market value of the underlying assets (bonds and equities) leads to the need to rebalance currency hedges. While this practice meets the customer reporting requirements it does little for an orderly market.

Another time to focus on is 1500 London time (referred to as New York cut) which is when most European-style options expire.

IMPACT OF CENTRAL BANK INTERVENTION

We looked in detail at central bank intervention and its impact in chapter 2, such that it is not necessary to cover it again here. The most active players in recent years have been the Swiss National Bank (SNB) and the Japanese (BOJ).

BREACH OF TECHNICAL LEVELS

Market moves can also be driven by technical factors. Technical analysis has an impact when key technical levels are breached because this can prompt increased buying or selling from traders, depending on the direction of the breach. These technical levels are usually well known in the market, such as the 200-day moving average or Fibonacci levels. These moves can be amplified by the buying and selling activity of funds that are model-based, utilising algorithms or econometric techniques to enter or exit the market when certain levels are hit.

SEASONAL PRICE PATTERNS

It is useful to be aware of seasonal price patterns. A notable example of this is the yen and the impact of US Treasury coupon (interest) payments. Four times a year, in February, May, August, and November, the US Treasury market concentrates redemption and coupon payments. The impact in the foreign exchange markets can be fairly significant, although it is not always. This involves specifically the coupon payments rather than the redemptions. Japanese fund managers represent a major percentage of overseas holders of US Treasuries. Redemption proceeds are normally hedged (or matched with new issuance) but coupon payments are not. Japanese fund managers have tended to use these coupon payments as current income and sell for yen after the money has been paid into their accounts.

DRAMATIC EVENTS

Despite any amount of planning and market knowledge, unexpected, tumultuous events – such as wars, terrorist attacks and natural disasters – can occur at any time and are capable of dramatically moving markets. It is worth noting that markets under stress will buy what are considered safe haven currencies, such as the Swiss franc.

This was dramatically illustrated by price movement of EUR/CHF following the terrorist attacks on the US 9/11 – the price chart is shown in Figure 9.1. The CHF made gains for nearly two weeks after the event as extreme uncertainty prevailed. In the absence of further attacks and economic assessment the markets steadied and CHF gains were pared back. The price action reflects the triggering of stop losses and poor liquidity, both of which I discuss in this book.

Figure 9.1 – Impact of 9/11 attack on CHF

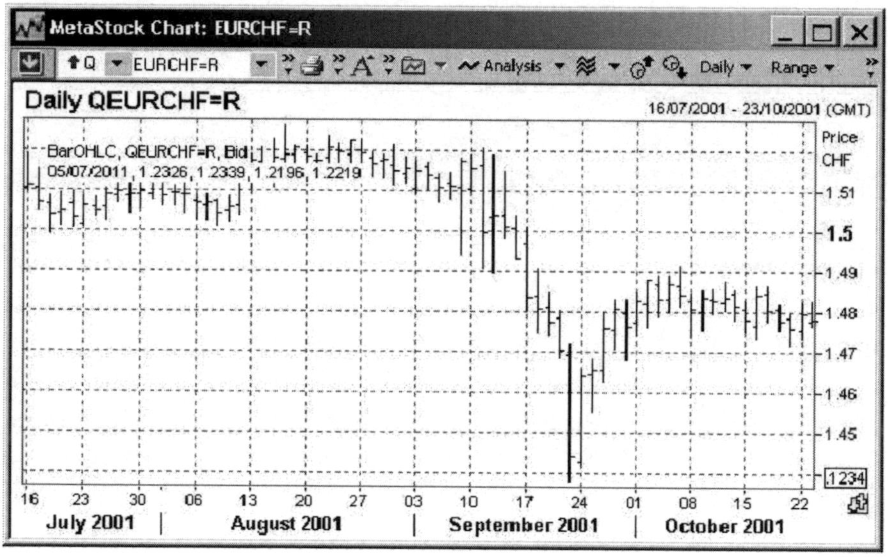

Source: Reuters

It is very difficult to consistently make money in foreign exchange and I have seen from experience that more people fail than succeed. As I have shown, there are numerous considerations, some complex, that have to be weighed and assessed. Moreover, events happen in real time leaving little time for reflection.

That being said, there is real scope to make money in foreign exchange. It is the most liquid market in the world – you can buy and, importantly, sell, at virtually anytime. There will always be opportunities.

MARKET INTELLIGENCE

This is a crucial influence on foreign exchange markets. Flow information is very important in what is essentially an over-the-counter market where there is no exchange-based information. For traders, the best source of market intelligence comes from observing supply and demand from customers. Who is doing what and why will form the basis for foreign exchange decision making. Where are the orders in the market and in what size? This is one reason why the pursuit of foreign exchange volume has formed the basis of the major trading banks' business models over the past 30 years. Indeed, as we noted earlier, to the extent that foreign exchange is dominated by less than ten banks. This information is a major attraction to large corporates/funds/central banks and can be pivotal to a dealing relationship. In this way volume begets volume.

10.

A BLUEPRINT FOR TRADING

n this chapter I will present a blueprint for successful trading. These are not rules as such, as this would suggest that if followed success would inevitably be the outcome. Nonetheless, trading is a skill which can be taught, even if success can never be guaranteed. To begin, while there are a number of ways to approach trading, the key component is the practitioner.

The starting point is therefore to make an honest self-assessment. Do you have the emotional inclination and resolve to trade? Are you prepared to pull the trigger or disciplined enough to take a loss? Many individuals start on the basis that it is easy. People reason that they have been successful in their business careers so why should they not be successful at foreign exchange? It comes as a shock to the ego that it is not so simple; a great deal of expertise is required and it is mentally wearing and time consuming.

I will start by noting a number of considerations you should take into account before you place a trade, during the time that the trade is active, and after a trade has been closed out.

BEFORE, DURING AND AFTER THE TRADE

You might think some of the points noted here are rather obvious but it is remarkable how often they are ignored. Some observations are clearly focused on the private client but will be applicable to most foreign exchange practitioners. As will become clear, most of the work is done before the trade is struck.

Before the trade

Treat trading as a business (of making money), not a hobby. It requires your full attention. You will build up an instinctive reference library more powerful than any technical or statistical construct. Important questions to ask yourself are:

- *Do you understand the product or structure that you are using?* If not, do not deal. It is vital to understand the nature of any financial instrument in the market place and what its risks and potential rewards are.

Moreover, buying into a complex structure can hide a host of profit margins that are embedded within it. Always check costs/fees.

- *How much risk are you willing to take on?* In other words, what is your pain barrier? Set it before, not after, the event. It is an unfortunate truth that losses come from what you expect the least.

- *Set realistic expectations.* Delusion is channelled into take-profit and stop loss scenarios. I shall be devoting some space later on how to approach losses. Unfortunately the old dealing mantra still holds: traders are generally too quick to take profits and too slow to take losses.

- *Look for books by traders who cover how they have lost money.* This will give you an idea of the mistakes you should avoid.

- There is a natural tendency to concentrate activity on the familiar. This applies to all forms of investment. The usual answer is to only trade what you follow or understand. This is the correct approach, but *don't narrow your trading opportunities through lack of research.*

- *Calculate how a given movement in the spot will impact your profit and loss account.* For example, in GBP/USD a 20 pip move in a GBP 1m position will impact your profit and loss by USD 2000. This focuses the mind.

- *Plan the trade, its entry and exit, before making the trade.* Use multiple outcomes in this process. Markets will always surprise so contingency plans are essential for a variety of situations, however unexpected.

- *Review technical support and resistance levels and be aware of perceived significant breakout levels.* Even if you don't believe in technical trading yourself, other people do and many traders will leave orders around perceived key levels.

- Check the calendar of *key events and news releases that can move the foreign exchange markets* and get a feel for expectations.

- *Establish how the prices from the bank are being generated.* This is important whether they are taken from a platform or direct from a salesperson. In other words, what is your cost of dealing? This is effectively measured against prime interbank rates (the rates at which the major banks will deal with each other). This can be viewed as the spread between the bid and offer when a two-way price is provided or simply the spread against the side requested.

- *Establish at the outset what limits your bank has set up for you.* There may be restrictions on how far forward you can deal. If trading on margin, understand what the margin requirement is for each new position.

- *Record the main details of every transaction.* This includes entry and exit prices, limit and stop loss orders, and the reason for the trade. Record times of trading and coincidence with major data releases. Traders are not machines and some perform better at different times of day.

- *Find out whether the bank will provide prices in all conditions and whether the dealing size will shrink if liquidity fails.* Do you have a bank for all seasons?

- *Ensure that your dealing counterparty is creditworthy.* Events of 2007-09 showed that some banks are more creditworthy than others and while the incidence of bank default on foreign exchange contracts is minimal, it is worth checking this area.

- *Does the trade give me a yield or is there a running (carry) cost in holding the position?*

- *Month-end can be a volatile time, especially if there have been sharp movements in the equity and bond markets.* If, for instance, there has been a rally in US asset markets this in effect increases the USD exposure of foreign portfolio investors and may prompt USD sales (hedge) to bring this exposure back in line.

- *Look for extreme trading divergence against historical levels and extreme overvaluation or undervaluation on PPP or fair value models.* Examples of this are GBP/USD above 1.90, the Norwegian Krona versus Swedish Krona around 1.25 (Norway overvalued), and Australian dollar versus New Zealand dollar around 1.30 (Australian dollar overvalued).

Timing a trade

There is no best time to trade, whether morning, afternoon, a particular day in the week, or on a full moon. I dealt with a large oil company who were convinced that Friday afternoon after 3.30 pm was the optimum time to trade cable. I never managed to convince them otherwise.

Certainly, it is not advisable to open a new trade ahead of important economic releases or central bank announcements or indeed Friday afternoons before a US holiday, especially if there has been a lot of price movement during the week, but this comes down to trading style and many successful trades are made on doing just this.

Many prefer to be reactive rather than try to lead. In this context have some understanding, as best you can, of market positioning of the currency involved, e.g., International Monetary Market (IMM). The IMM data is the CFTC (Chicago Futures Commitment of Traders) Report. This data examines the net futures positions (long contracts minus short contracts) of non-commercial traders on the exchange. This is published weekly; the IMM data is only available against the dollar. If the market is already extremely long the room for appreciation is more difficult without a new catalyst. Similarly, if the market is extremely short, the scope for further losses will be limited.

In Japan the TFX (Tokyo Financial Exchange) is closely watched for Japanese retail positioning. There are plenty of others to view also. For instance, Barclays Group BTOP FX Index seeks to replicate the overall composition of the currency sector of the managed futures industry with regard to trading style and overall market exposure. Mercer Currency Manager Index tracks the performance of a group of currency managers chosen by Mercer from Deutsche Bank's FXSelect Platform.

Correlations

Look for correlations. For a period following Lehman's collapse (2008) there was a negative correlation between the Standard & Poor's 500 Index and the yen – weak equities pointed to yen strength. This was also the case with the dollar. In the wake of the Fed talking US short-term rates close to zero, the dollar was increasingly popular as a funding currency to fund risk portfolios and as such became highly sensitive to whether investors were expanding or reducing leverage. The more normal correlation would be with bond yields, i.e., higher US yields dollar supportive. Another example of a strong correlation is sterling versus the financials. Data from January 2006 to January 2010 shows about a 96% correlation between the UK leading banks' shares and the sterling trade-weighted index.

There is a group of currencies that come under the commodity currency umbrella, including Australia, Canada, New Zealand and Norway. This nomenclature is determined by a country's dependence on commodity exports and as such there is a positive correlation with the Commodity

Research Bureau Index (CRB). There is a particular dollar bias in commodity markets as commodities are priced in dollars, and this leads to a strong link between dollar and commodity performance. As a general rule commodity up trends are associated with a declining dollar and vice versa. Again, this correlation can be erratic, particularly when commodities are extremely volatile as was the case in 2008-09.

Unfortunately correlations, just like trading ranges, have a finite shelf life. Seasonal trading patterns fit within this context. For instance, there is a market perception that the Japanese fiscal year-end (end of March) tends to be a time of yen strength against the US dollar. However, the evidence suggests the opposite. USD/JPY tends to strengthen about two weeks before the year-end and continues to strengthen into the first week of the new fiscal year. This seasonal bias turns USD negative in the second week of the new year and for the next two weeks virtually reverses the year-end gain. The strongest period for the JPY tends to be the period between mid-February and mid-March (and also during August).

Once the trade has been placed

- *Stay within your risk tolerance – don't leave a stop loss and then move the order as soon as the price approaches.* Obviously no one wants to be stopped out but you have to turn it into a positive decision not a failure. It is an act of discipline and keeps you in the game.

- *What is your reward to money at risk ratio?* This represents the ratio of the number of pips a trader is looking to profit versus the number of pips they are risking. Ideally the ratio should be greater than 1. For instance, a trader who sets a limit order 100 pips from entry and a stop loss 50 pips from entry is employing a 2:1 reward to risk ratio (100/50). This can be regarded as a conservative position. A trader who sets a limit order 100 pips from entry and a stop loss 300 pips from entry, a ratio of 1:3, is making an aggressive one-way trade, and this is not recommended.

- *Don't overtrade.* There is no need to chase trades. Opportunities will always come; taking a break is not a sign of failure.

- *Don't try to fight the market.* If central banks fail with their interventions, what chance do you have?

- *Assess market moves.* Attempt to ascertain whether they are order driven, e.g., around fixings, or M&A (mergers and acquisitions) related, or directional. In other words short-term, versus medium-term trend flows.

- Especially after key economic releases, *do not get seduced by the initial reaction* in the foreign exchange market. Sometimes a more accurate assessment can be observed in the bond markets. Don't get tunnel vision.

After the trade has been closed out

- *Assess the outcome.* What went right? What went wrong?

- *Reassess your mindset.*

- *Record everything.*

MANAGING LOSSES

The key to making money in foreign exchange is learning how to manage your losses. Perfect trading records simply don't happen – trading should be viewed as a percentage game and with that comes profits and losses. Any trader can afford to take losses provided that they are contained. In fact, some have gone as far as to say that traders "should learn to love" losses.[9]

This notion is firmly based in behavioural studies. As I suggested above, there is a tendency to take profits too early and losses too slowly (disposition effect). The former is a way to validate success; the latter relates to pride and regret. If a number of trades in different currency pairs are running at the same time, with one trade in profit and another in loss, the tendency is to close out the one in profit.

The idea of running losses too long is one thing, but there is also the phenomenon of adding more risk to a loss-making situation in order to retrieve the position. This is usually known as 'doubling up' or 'averaging'. Apart from simply losing money, an extended loss leaves mental scars and can have a profound effect on a trader's decision making. Trading requires confidence – doubts over decision making will result in missed trading opportunities.

The most common technique to control losses is the stop loss order. This is how the professional market has traded for years. Traders generally have loss limits, some per trade, some intra-day or even a month. The situation every private trader is afraid of is that the stop loss order will be filled, the trade stopped out, and then suddenly the price direction reverses again in the direction of the trade. I have had plenty of instructions to move or cancel a stop because it was getting too close, just for this reason.

Stop loss orders do tend to congregate and it is somewhat galling that everyone in the market seems to know where they are. There is a natural interest to hunt these stops, trigger them and then take advantage of the ensuing price action. However, whether you are a professional or a private trader losses have to be contained. In the former case, loss of employment follows, and in the latter, the erosion of capital will eventually take you out of the game.

---

[9] Gerald Ashley, *Financial Speculation* (Harriman House).

Managing losses is not all about placing stop loss orders, it can be just as much about managing the level of activity. Overtrading is dangerous. The level of dealing activity has to be allied with the degree of volatility in that currency pair or indeed of the market itself. In a volatile market it would be appropriate to not only reduce the level of activity but more importantly the size of the trade. In a volatile market a GBP 1m position can equate to a GBP 3m position in a quiet market. By simply adjusting down your position size in a volatile market, you level the playing field for yourself.

INVESTMENT VS. SPECULATION

In the general lexicon, there is the idea that *investment* – putting money or effort into something to develop it – is good, while *speculation* is a pejorative term, suggesting avaricious risk-takers operating outside the wider social interest.

The notion that investment is good has possibly something to do with time. The idea of investing for future growth has for many an emotional attraction, or it signals prudence and informed decision making. The idea of making a profit intra-day – as a speculator might seek to do – suggests seat-of-the-pants decision making or even sharp practice.

However, even though it may make people uncomfortable, we are essentially talking about the same activity when we use the terms 'investment' and 'speculation', both operate under the umbrella of uncertainty, a characteristic of all financial markets. What differentiates them is how risk is measured. This has proved to be a subjective and contentious issue.

Gambling is fundamentally different as it operates with defined and known probabilities.

11.
LIQUIDITY

The definition of 'liquidity' is when currency can be bought or sold quickly (or within an expected period of time) with minimal loss of price (minimal price effects) and at any time within market hours. Liquidity relates to the certainty of price and time. Therefore, we can view liquidity risk as the degree to which we are surprised by the value and time outcome. The key element of a liquid market is that there is a large pool of buyers and sellers at all times. The importance of understanding liquidity cannot be overstated. This analysis is transferable to any asset.

Liquidity has always been a talking point amongst traders. The focus is very rarely on liquid markets but rather on illiquid trading conditions. The latter are often used to rationalise unexplained market moves and indeed losses. It may seem strange to talk of illiquidity in the foreign exchange market, where daily turnover is approximately USD 4trn, but it does occur. In the foreign exchange market, currencies will have their own liquidity characteristics, which inevitably plays a major part in our trading decisions. Liquidity can be measured by how often a currency is bought and sold, in other words volume traded. In the foreign exchange market this is an after-the-event statistic as no live figures are generated. However, one can sometimes sense when volumes are down from noticing erratic price action and from anecdotal market comments.

The importance of liquidity is that it provides the basis for an orderly market. Without liquidity it becomes more difficult to match buyers and sellers and transactions become less efficient, and prices can become distorted. I use the word 'distorted' as there is no correct price in practice. Contrary to some academic commentators I think changes in liquidity conditions are readily observed, although it is true that some price movements are not easily assigned to this state of affairs. To date, most trading models do not attempt to factor in liquidity.

Examples of currencies which are prone to illiquidity are the Norwegian krona and New Zealand dollar. This is a function of the number of participants and the size of their economies. The Scandinavians also, for instance, take a month off in the summer, which can make trading in the currencies of these countries difficult at this time.

Holidays in other countries can have a massive impact, too. The obvious are US holidays, especially Thanksgiving, as many people return home. Christmas and New Year affects everyone, with so many different holiday practices around the world. In the Far East there is the Chinese New Year celebration and in Japan Golden Week holidays. In all these examples, it should not be assumed that there will be large erratic price actions. On many occasions one can go to sleep and wake with prices practically unchanged.

On a regular basis one sees liquidity swings on a Friday afternoon as traders withdraw and positions developed during the week are squared up, especially as many holidays follow on a Monday. Moreover, if we also have the 1600hrs fix and month-end this can generate a volatile liquidity cocktail. At this time funds will look to rebalance their currency holdings in their portfolios and will trade these adjustments against rates set at 1600hrs.

ASSESSING LIQUIDITY

In assessing liquidity we can refer to a number of indicators. *Market depth* measures the size of an order needed to change the price significantly, or can be looked at as the size of an order that can be converted without affecting the price. For example, EUR/USD is the most liquid currency pair in foreign exchange and virtually all banks will trade this pair. On one occasion I was involved in the purchase of EUR 800m and this did not move the price. This is sometimes referred to as 'a deep market' in academic texts (not in the market); a deep market is also a liquid market. Intuitively you can see the advantage of having this order. If buying EUR 800m does not move the price higher then there must be considerable selling interest. I therefore should look to sell.

Another useful indicator is termed *market breadth*, which in practice is the spread between the bid and offer (ask) price. This is sometimes referred to as 'market tightness' and indicates the cost of turning a position around (buy and sell). Individual currency pairs will have a *normal* spread for a given size of transaction. When these spreads widen (which is easily visible with modern pricing platforms) it is a good sign that liquidity is deteriorating. When the spreads become narrower it is an indication that liquidity is improving. Quite simply, it indicates volume and the presence of many buyers and sellers. A widening of spreads also indicates that price volatility is on the rise and reflects the lack of participation in the market. We shall look at some extreme examples of this later.

Allied to a normal market spread is the notion of a *normal market size*. A price quoted is expected to support a certain size of transaction. Again this will vary from currency to currency but deviations away from the norm will suggest a change in liquidity conditions. Markets provide liquidity and liquidity involves both time and quantity.

The issue of time is an interesting one. If one is selling a house the liquidity time is quite different; a month would generally be considered very quick. In the foreign exchange market a minute might be considered a long time. That is why in my definition I used the phrase *expected* time. This will be determined by the size of the transaction and the currency involved.

Speed of execution is a characteristic of liquidity but not a necessary condition. I may have a huge buy order of EUR which may be completed in a few minutes. However, this may simply be a reflection that the market is a one-way seller, which by my definition does not constitute a liquid market. There must be buyers and sellers punctuating the pricing ladder for there to be liquidity.

To take a graphic example, in 1992 the Bank of England was probably the only buyer of sterling in town and when they withdrew, sterling suffered a precipitous fall. Without liquidity there is little point in trading in the market via various trading platforms. They would not be able to trade in size on the prices shown. Indeed at the height of the banking crisis in 2009 banks reverted to direct calling.

WHEN LIQUIDITY DISAPPEARS

In recent years there have been a number of occasions when liquidity by any definition has all but disappeared. The most notable was around the Lehman Brothers collapse in 2008

Risk aversion was extreme and there was a flight to safe haven assets with US Treasuries (US dollar) the major beneficiary, followed by the Swiss franc. There was also the exit from carry trades (which are dealt with in more detail below). These were borrowings in very low interest rate currencies (primarily Swiss francs and yen) with the proceeds converted into currencies with higher interest rates (e.g., sterling) or to fund equities or other risk assets. The exit was brutal; the trouble was that there was not enough liquidity for everyone to exit their positions.

Professor Avi Persaud and Professor Michael Mainelli talk of *liquidity black holes*. This is an excellent description of what occurred in the carry trade. Persaud says "a liquidity black hole is where price falls do not bring out buyers, but generate even more sellers." This is contrary to normal market understanding where price falls would expect to attract buyers. As Brandon Davies points out, in a black hole "he who panics first, panics best". In foreign exchange a great deal of this panic can be generated out of black box computer trading models.

In other words, computer–driven trading models will dictate the trading and, in this case, exit levels. Stop loss orders are a feature of the foreign exchange market as traders are limited on the loss positions that they can run. They can seem randomly located but in many instances they can be placed at key technical levels. A break would suggest further losses and encourage further selling, certainly the case in 2009.

A foreign exchange black hole has a relatively short life as buyers emerge looking for a base, or correction level, after a sharp fall. This can be a false dawn as a rally in the price merely encourages further selling, which in turn stops out the bargain hunters. Throughout this process dealing prices widen (the bid-offer spread) as traders' uncertainty and risk increases.

The opposite of a liquidity black hole is referred to as a *liquidity white bubble*. This is where price rises do not bring out sellers, but generate even more buyers. This price action is rare in foreign exchange.

The foreign exchange markets are increasingly susceptible to liquidity disruptions and this can be attributed to a number of factors. First, as discussed above, there has been a significant concentration of foreign exchange business. Global markets are now so well interlinked, liquidity problems in one asset class can impact across the entire asset class spectrum. For instance, there has been strong correlation between the credit and equity markets and foreign exchange over the past few years. The foreign exchange market uses similar analytics and information systems, which increases the likelihood of similar trading strategies. Also, with increased use of performance benchmarking, trading is tending to be concentrated at various fixing times during the day.

So liquidity is good and illiquidity is bad. In a liquid market many trades can be transacted with moderate price impact. This is generally a better environment for dealers to make money. I should note that I am not talking about static prices when it is nigh impossible to make money. In illiquid markets dealers will normally transact fewer trades and with greater risk. However, this is not always the case as the bank may be unwilling to take the customer foreign exchange risk on. Instead the bank will work the order, looking for buyers or sellers.

In an illiquid market there are fewer buyers and sellers and the amounts traded are reduced so an order could take some time to fill. In this case banks can make considerable profits with no risk under the cloak of an illiquid, thin or simply difficult market. A good example of this is Christmas Eve. It is therefore important for the customer, if possible, to time their transaction with a mind to potential liquidity conditions. My last reflection on liquidity is that economic bubbles (and their inevitable collapse) are largely constructed by overly expansive monetary policies of central banks.

As mentioned above, an infamous example of a liquidity black hole surrounded the mass exit from carry trades in 2007 and 2009. It is instructive to look at these events in more detail.

THE CARRY TRADE AND TORSCHLUSSPANIK (DOOR SHUT PANIC)

The carry trade is borrowing funds from banks in low interest currencies – in recent history, principally the yen and Swiss franc – and then using the money to invest in assets such as property, equities, commodities and bonds. During the 2000s, up to 2008, everybody from multinational corporations and major banks to private individuals were involved.

Figure 11.1 shows the growth of the carry trade from 2000 to 2007, as illustrated by sterling versus yen. As the banker Martin put it in 1720, when subscribing to South Sea stock at the top of the market: "When the rest of the world are mad, we must imitate them in some measure."

Figure 11.1 – The rise and rise of the carry trade 2001-2007

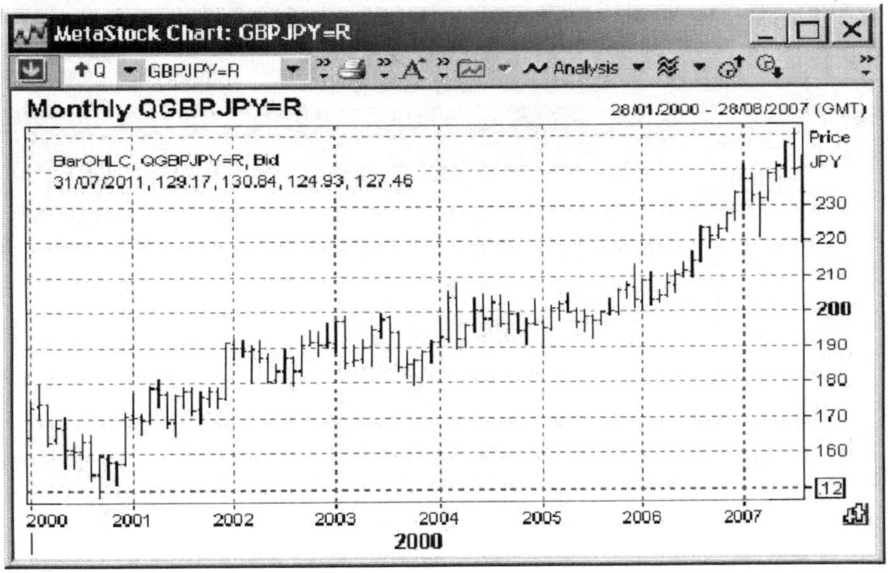

Source : Reuters

For the carry trade to operate a number of conditions need to be satisfied.

First, the funding currencies need to have low real interest rates and there needs to be an expectation that this will persist for a reasonable length of time. Following the 2007-09 financial crisis, central banks in many of the world's major economies have slashed interest rates to stave off recession and further bank failures, so investors are spoilt for choice when it comes to choose a funding currency, but of course there are now fewer high yielding currencies.

Second, high liquidity is crucial in the funding currency because it makes it easier for investors to fund their trades. Third, the carry trade is attractive in low volatility as this will keep the capital at risk broadly stable while benefiting from the difference in interest rates. If the interest rate differential is low there is far less yield protection against adverse market moves and so investors are far more sensitive to changes in volatility. If there is a high carry, as for instance there was between sterling and the yen, then there is greater tolerance to underlying moves in the spot.

There was a long build up in the carry trades during the 2000s, but the collapse was relatively brief and brutal, as can be seen in Figure 11.2. This price action encapsulates a number of topics I have discussed, namely the stop loss, liquidity in a black hole, and also human nature.

Figure 11.2 – The end of the game 2007-09

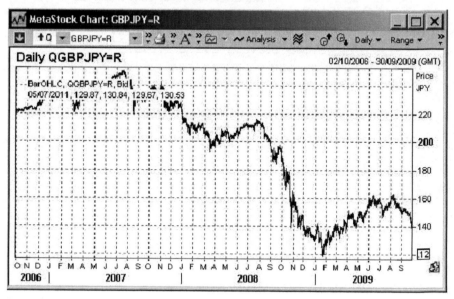

Source: Reuters

As the carry trade is funded by capital borrowed from banks to invest in other assets, with the assets invested in providing security for the loans, when asset prices fall so does the bank's security. At some point there will be forced asset sales as loan to value ratios break agreed levels, or if the borrower is unwilling to provide additional collateral. A collapse in global equity prices in 2007-08, with loans called in, and a flight to US Treasuries and other safe haven repatriations, led to an unwinding of carry trades producing an unbreakable spiral. Foreign exchange in this case was not driving the asset markets – it was quite the reverse.

Risk aversion and uncertainty are the key enemies of the carry trade and with the collapse in bank equity and the worst recession since the 1930s, there was plenty to latch on to. In the past few years the carry trade has been highly correlated with equity performance although this has not been the case historically. As market sentiment improves, this correlation should break down. Eventually, memories of the 2007-08 collapse will fade and the carry trade will grow in popularity again. Some may argue that this point has already been reached, with the US dollar the primary funding currency and the emerging markets the investment destination of choice.

12.

HEDGING CURRENCY EXPOSURE

OVERVIEW OF HEDGING

This chapter will highlight the importance of currency hedging to companies and portfolio managers. Hedging is a tactic used to offset losses or potential losses that might arise from exposure to currencies. A perfect hedge eliminates the possibility of future gain or loss. It may be said that the point of hedging is to achieve some measure of certainty in an uncertain world. The idea is to manage exposure on this basis, not towards a particular forecast.

From a corporate point of view, if a company generates cash flows in currencies other than the base currency of the country in which it is based, then the value of the company will fluctuate with movements in the exchange rates of the various currencies. Whether or not this risk is accepted – i.e., left unhedged, or actively removed - i.e., hedged – can have a significant impact on the long-term success of the company.

Pension funds, hedge funds, central banks, sovereign wealth funds and private client portfolios invest globally and as a result are exposed to assets denominated in a wide range of currencies. For example, a UK-based investor who makes a 10% allocation to Japanese equities has a 10% exposure to the Japanese yen. I will provide a brief insight into how fund managers can approach the issue of hedging.

I shall be posing a lot of questions which need to be addressed in order to establish the correct process. However, once the exposure and objectives have been defined the final criterion is risk appetite.

The overall approach is just as relevant to the high net worth private clients who tend to ignore currency risk or receive little advice on the subject.

SOURCES OF EXPOSURE

A key role for the corporate Treasurer is to identify where there is currency exposure and to determine the extent of hedging required. The following are the most common sources of currency exposure.

Transaction examples

- Payables/Receivables
- Inter-company loans
- Dividends/Royalties
- Acquisitions/Divestures

Hedging this type of exposure is usually obligatory under a company's treasury policies and usually achieved via the forward foreign exchange market. Acquisitions or bid situations are sometimes handled using options. The Prudential bid for AIG Asia 2010 was reportedly dealt in this manner, but in fact the acquisition came to nothing.

Translation examples

- Foreign assets, liabilities and equity
- Reported income from overseas subsidiaries

Protection of the foreign currency profits of overseas businesses can bring some certainty to consolidated profits but is generally not done further than 12 months in advance. This is in part a practical issue since obtaining foreign exchange facilities beyond one year is difficult, but also taking a view on future performance can be as challenging as taking a view on the exchange rate. Cost, however, unless one is taking the option route, is not really a significant consideration.

Fluctuations in the value of overseas' net assets usually flows into the consolidated balance sheet through shareholders' funds. It does not affect cash flow. A common way to hedge this is simply to borrow in the foreign currency the net asset value. So changes in the balance sheet value of the net assets are offset by changes in the value of the net debt. However, there are potential issues attached to this type of hedge. The extra borrowing may impact on the ability to borrow (raise capital) for other purposes through, for example, increased gearing and it may raise the cost of overall borrowing.

THE HEDGING PROCESS

The actual hedging transaction and the instrument chosen only comes after a series of questions has been addressed. Virtually all the work comes in the planning. Once the exposure and objectives have been defined the final criterion for how hedging is employed is risk appetite.

Define exposures

While balance sheet hedging is important, especially to accountants, my focus is on managing cash flow. Without positive cash flow the company will not function. The first point to consider is what is your base currency. This for most is pretty straightforward but it is worth having a look at your business to see which currency has a dominant influence on your activities.

The next task is to estimate the net foreign currency cash flow. Note the word 'net'; can the currencies be netted? For example, EUR 5m of sales against EUR 3m of costs will generate a net requirement of only EUR 2m.

Dates are not as important as you would expect; as we have shown, foreign exchange contracts are easily moved. However, allow for flexibility in timing of commitments. This is more relevant to option contracts.

Cash flow reliability has an obvious bearing on the decision process and the following questions should be addressed:

- Is it certain in so far as it is contractual?
- Are some of the cash flows more certain than others?
- Is there a seasonal bias?
- Is there flexibility of receipt of cash flows?

When the net cash flow has been estimated – there is no reason to stop at one year, go for as far as you reasonably can – add on some sensitivity analysis. This will show the impact of certain movements in the exchange rate.

Define objectives

Must there be a guaranteed worst case? What happens if this level is breached? As we have seen, stop loss orders and options can provide worst case protection. However, there are circumstances where the market rate has moved against you since the budget rate was set. If your worst case level has been breached, is it permissible to hedge forward at a worst level than budget?

What is your risk appetite? Do you always look to cover 100% of known exposures? How far forward would you cover? Do you cover newly identified exposures immediately? Is there an obligation to hedge forward if the market is in your favour?

Which instruments internally are allowed for hedging purposes and is there a budget for this? Are the staff sufficiently trained to deal in these instruments?

Once the exposure and objectives have been defined the process of choosing an appropriate hedging instrument is relatively easy. Often the number of appropriate hedging instruments available is small.

For example, take a hedge fund operating in London. Income (and profit) is predominantly in USD and expenses are in sterling. Every month the hedge fund pays out rent, salaries and utilities. Every month it receives a management fee in USD. This management fee is fixed under contract and is spread over a number of investors. The conservative instinct is to cover the sterling running costs, especially if the exchange rate is well within the budget/break-even level.

The simplest and arguably the most economical approach is to enter into monthly forward contracts. If Treasury policy is to set the hedge duration for 12 months then 12 contracts will be agreed at the outset with every contract at maturity being replaced – a 12-month rolling hedge.

This method is very common and is liked because it is cheap, flexible (amounts and duration can be varied if there is a change in view or rate), provides certainty of cash flow and is in effect an averaging process. When GBP/USD was trading around 2 a few years ago a number of clients bought *Armageddon* options which were way out of the money and as such were considered cheap. This was to protect future income/profits. Uncertain income streams and positions which are under water lend themselves to option structures. In the latter case the other alternatives are to do nothing or to realise the loss.

IMPACT OF HEDGING

For corporates, funds or any organisation that is required to publish accounts there is a potential impact to hedging. This relates to the profit and loss effect of marking to market hedges whether they be forward contracts or options of any complexity. Mark to market will value the contract at current prices on a daily basis, and, in this context, measures the effectiveness of the hedge. It also can create huge volatility in earnings. You may think that if an option has no intrinsic value the problem has gone away but remember it can still have time value.

Inevitably the accounting treatment can be very complex and should be understood and implemented prior to dealing. There will be initial and ongoing documentation requirements, for instance cataloguing foreign exchange and option (derivative) contracts, including embedded derivatives. There has to be in the end acceptance of some earnings impact to achieve financial/economic hedging objectives.

Another impact is that the currency hedge is implemented through rolling forward contracts and these can remove most, if not all, of the currency risk within a portfolio, depending on the hedge ratio and tenor chosen. This risk reduction, through forwards, does come with cash flow implications, as we saw earlier when looking at rolling forward strategies.

CURRENCY OVERLAY

What is currency overlay?

Despite the move to a floating exchange rate system in the 1970s, and increased volatility in foreign exchange prices, the portfolio manager has only focused their mind on how to deal with currency risk since the early 1990s. This interest may be due to the greater attention that began to be paid to short-term performance and to increased cross-border flows of investment funds.

At this time specialists began to provide disciplined currency management services to fund managers with international investment portfolios. In essence they separated the management of currency risk from the asset allocation and security selection process. They became known as 'currency overlay managers'.

At one end of the spectrum, currency overlay means that currency risk is fully hedged (passive approach). At the other end, it means that currency is viewed as a separate asset class and positions are taken to maximise potential gains in the underlying currencies (active approach).

The overlay manager and the portfolio manager operate in parallel. The portfolio manger buys and sells international equities, bonds, etc., with reference only to their investment merits. The decision is independent of currency views. The overlay manager will analyse the currency exposures generated by these activities and will decide on how best, if at all, to hedge these exposures. The other fund manager's activities continue unaffected. Currency hedging is therefore, in effect, overlaid on the portfolios.

Although avoiding all currency risk is considered a better strategy than being fully exposed, some currency exposure is viewed as beneficial to capture additional diversification benefits. The ratio of hedged to unhedged currency exposure is called the 'hedging ratio'. A trader would typically choose a constant hedge ratio based on historical data and a specific view to the future.

The overlay manager will be looking at this hedge ratio on a regular basis. Some will actively manage this but typically it is at month or quarter end that adjustments are made. When there have been significant moves during the period this can generate volatile price action at this time.

The overlay manager will make and execute currency trading decisions on behalf of the investor. The investor remains the beneficial owner of all contracts executed by the overlay manger and all profit or loss from the contracts is for the client's account.

The mandate agreed with the client will determine the risk the currency overlay manager can take and the instruments that may be used to implement this. Targets can be set for a currency manager to either minimise risk or maximise return.

Optimal hedging approaches for overlay/portfolio managers

The optimal hedge ratio to employ will vary from asset to asset but is broadly determined by the following three factors:

1. The higher the currency volatility, relative to the underlying asset, the greater the need to hedge the currency risk. In these circumstances the investment has effectively become more of a currency play rather than a predominant view on the asset.

The volatility of currencies tends to be significantly higher than that of bonds. As a result, unhedged global bond exposures are more influenced by currency movements than by bond price movements, and are in greater need of hedging. Equity volatility, however, tends to be higher than currency volatility. As a result, currency movements have a lesser impact on equity returns and therefore hedging an equity position against foreign exchange exposure is less important. Some funds view 75% as an optimal hedge ratio for global equities and 100% for global bonds in the absence of currency views.

2. The higher the correlation between the underlying asset and the currency the greater the need for hedging currency exposure as diversification benefits are reduced. Currencies that are uncorrelated with the underlying asset can help reduce volatility in a similar fashion to which investing in uncorrelated asset classes helps diversify portfolios.

3. The difference in interest rates between the currencies; currencies with high interest rates are more expensive to hedge. In the (forward) hedging process the fund will receive or pay the difference in interest rates between the two currencies.

Arguments against currency overlay

- Currency trading is a zero sum game – it is not statistically possible to come out ahead consistently.

- Currency movements represent a random walk and are unpredictable.

- There are no opportunities that come from investing in an efficient, liquid foreign exchange market.

Arguments for currency overlay

Currency has a substantial impact on risk and return in global investment portfolios. Investors with foreign assets are exposed to two major risks: the price of the asset may fall and the price of the currency in which it is quoted may fall. The currency risk can be as large as the asset price risk and is more unpredictable. In some instances fund managers have little incentive to manage that risk as the benchmarks assume unhedged currency risk.

The notion of a zero sum game and no expected long-term return imply that currencies follow purchasing power parity over time. However, we have seen under floating exchange rate systems that divergence from equilibrium levels can be extreme and indeed can take many years to return to equilibrium levels (if at all). Not all fund managers can wait for years in cases when their investors have a much shorter time horizon. The overlay manager can pre-empt these extreme moves by implementing a hedging strategy.

The assumption that foreign exchange markets are efficient is flawed. Under efficient market theory competing decision makers seek to maximise profits, utilising available information such that it is immediately incorporated into the price. In practice only a small group of participants fall into this category. There are a range of different motivations and objectives that do not match this ideal.

Investors buy or sell currency to purchase or dispose of foreign assets. The timing is usually driven by the price of the underlying asset or asset allocation decision, rarely by the price of the currency. Similarly, companies will buy or sell currency to meet cash flow requirements as they arise or to lock in a budgeted exchange rate for profits, or to protect trading margins. Central banks will buy or sell currency to meet international obligations or to satisfy policy goals related to the management of exchange rate levels or currency reserves. This interpretation of market trading – the absence in large part of profit maximisers – is very important to currency overlay as it supports the view that overlay managers can add value.

Choosing currency overlay managers

Clearly, currency views need to be correct for value to be added. It is important that the process is managed by knowledgeable and experienced staff, ideally with a successful proprietary or model trading background and expertise in all aspects of portfolio management. It is important to establish a disciplined trading methodology; this can be systemic, model-based or discretionary. The former approach is increasingly favoured. In this context, the creation of a suitable benchmark is essential as this should represent a true expression of the client's preferred balance between risk and reward in the foreign exchange market. Fees are inevitably an issue but a combination of a fixed management fee and a performance-related element is considered best practice.

In choosing any manager the focus will be on people, philosophy, process and performance. The first three should generate performance on a consistent basis.

Risk management is now all-important to the modern manager. A considerable amount of time is normally spent understanding the decision-making process, including who makes each decision and where ultimate accountability lies. Performance is clearly important but it is essential to have reports which can show how this is being generated to ascertain that the declared philosophy and style of the currency manager is being adhered to.

CONCLUSION

Currency exposure in investment portfolios needs to be identified and managed. This applies just as much to the individual high net worth private client as to the large fund.

13.

THE MANAGEMENT OF DEALING

Dealing in the foreign exchange market is not without its risks. History shows that large sums can be lost as well as made and consequently great care is needed in dealing. In the opening part of this chapter I shall identify the different types of risk that you will be exposed to in transacting foreign exchange. Clearly some of the risks are virtually impossible to quantify, such as fraud. The purpose, however, is to provide a checklist which at least will form a base from which to make an assessment of risk.

Allied to dealing risks is control and management of the dealing function and this is developed later in the chapter. The discussion is relevant to all practitioners of foreign exchange.

RISKS

Counterparty and settlement risk

All foreign exchange transactions involve dealing with someone else. As a result the quality of the counterparty is paramount since if the counterparty is not financially secure they will be unable to fulfil the obligation of settling the foreign exchange contract. This is why banks analyse the strength of their counterparties – corporate, banks, financial institutions and individuals – and why non-banks should analyse the strength of the bank.

At a time of this review a limit is usually established as to how much business a bank feels it prudent to transact with a particular counterparty.

The core of foreign exchange business is the transfer of very large sums of money around the world and making sure that both sides of the transaction settle.

The critical risk here is settlement risk – there is potential for 100% loss of the contract amount on the day of settlement if funds are paid away before receipt of cover and the counterparty goes bankrupt. For this reason many banks will limit the amount of foreign exchange which can be settled with any one counterparty on a single day.

If the counterparty fails before the day of settlement the bank will not settle the contract on the due date but will need to replace the cancelled contract for the same maturity date; then the mark-to-market profit and loss is at risk. For instance, if the customer has sold the bank GBP 5m, the bank will cover this in the market by selling GBP 5m. If there is no delivery of the GBP 5m to the bank on the settlement day it will have to go back into the market and buy GBP 5m. The risk to the bank is the difference between the exchange rate on the original contract and the exchange rate on the new contract.

Foreign exchange settlement risk is one of the biggest systemic risks to the financial markets and has been of particular interest to regulators since the collapse of Lehman Brothers 2008. This is continually being improved by the development of systems such as continuous linked settlement (CLS) where both sides' instructions for a foreign exchange trade are settled simultaneously. Currently however, only about 50% of daily global turnover is settled through CLS with the number of account users being around 5000.

Transfer risk

Transfer risk refers to a situation where a country closes its foreign exchange markets or imposes major restrictions. A number of Asian countries have made it extremely difficult to repatriate funds from their countries. The general practice is to prevent or restrict the sale of the domestic currency. Countries also exhaust their foreign currency reserves and while they can print domestic currency they cannot print foreign currency. Therefore, defaults or delays in payments can occur. In the post-war experience this has been most prevalent in South America, Africa and Asia.

Operational risk

Operational risk relates to delay or administrative error and is usually a function of inefficient systems or poorly trained operating staff. It can be monies paid late and/or on the wrong day and/or to the wrong place. While errors are regularly made it is the speed and attitude with which they are corrected that is important. I would suggest more corporate accounts have been moved because of persistent delays and errors than due to any pricing issue.

Liquidity risk

This recognises the ability to enter and exit trades with minimal loss of value and in a reasonable time period. Please refer to chapter 11 on liquidity.

Fraud

In recent times a number of major frauds, resulting in major losses, have made the news. Barings is the best known as it brought the bank down. Other recent examples can be drawn from France, America and Australia, but pick any country and you will find a fraud in its banking system at one point or another.

In most cases there is no initial motive of personal gain for the individual dealer. Rather, a pattern that recurs is a wrong position being created and the trader being unwilling to admit the error and choosing to hide it through various means in the belief that the position would come good. Of course, sometimes fraud is carried out with the aim of financial gain. This could be to enhance a bonus or possibly a bribe to execute a particular transaction. The latter has resonance when corporates deal.

Collusion amongst staff, whether it be between dealer and operations or dealer and management, is one way that a position can remain hidden; the other is simply that sometimes systems and control procedures (limits and supervision of personnel) are not up to the job. A structure has to be in place underpinned by well-trained and honest staff. The supervising staff have to fully understand the business that they are supervising.

DEALING LIMITS AT BANKS

Discipline is at the heart of all successful trading. The principles involved in placing limits on how banks can trade are readily transferable to funds, corporate and private individuals. First and foremost, limits are written to protect the bank, its shareholders and depositors. That being said, they need to be set up such that a dealing department can operate without undue bureaucracy.

Dealing limits will vary from bank to bank, depending upon the size, expertise and market activity of the bank concerned. The principles involved apply to all banks, from the largest to smallest institution. Limits are normally set by senior management in consultation with the Treasury department.

Limits should not be considered static; market conditions can vary, the bank will grow and customers and the type of business executed can change. It may therefore be necessary for limits to be increased or even reduced.

Setting up limits is one thing, but monitoring them effectively is another. In the past this was led by the chief dealer and treasurer but today it is largely in the hands of risk departments. These risk departments exist because it is important to understand how profits and losses have been made. Large profits deserve as much attention as large losses. Have the dealers been brilliant, been lucky or have they overtraded and abused limits?

In all dealing rooms, regardless of limits, losses will be made. The purpose of controls is to ensure that these are kept to an acceptable level and that bank procedures have not been ignored or trades hidden. Communication between management and the dealing department needs to be regular in order that a dealing strategy can be adapted to current market conditions and customer requirements.

Independent verification from knowledgeable staff is essential to ensure that policies and procedures are being adhered to.

Types of limits

*   *Trading limits*: This relates to the maximum amount of a particular currency that can be over-bought or over-sold. These can be exceeded during the day as the bank executes client trades but they are expected to be back within agreed levels as soon as practically possible. Usually,

there will be an overnight open position limit and an intra-day open position limit and that will tend to be the larger of the two. This not only applies to an individual currency but to the aggregate position for all currencies. This is the sum of all long currency positions plus the sum of all short currency positions. In practice there will be a major currency limit for USD, EUR, CHF, JPY (GBP), and a minor currency limit for AUD, CAD, DKK, HKD, NZD, NOK, SEK, ZAR, and others. Trades will only be allowed in specified currencies.

- *Gap limits*: These restrict the amounts which can be over-sold or over-bought in any one particular period or on a cumulative basis. This relates to the forward book and to the money market operations. It is generally felt that the longer the period the greater the risk, so exposure limits will vary with time, e.g., GBP 150m one month, GBP 50m six months. This could also vary with the currency where liquidity is an issue.

- *Maximum maturities*: Unless otherwise specified, limits for individual counterparties will normally allow trades up to one year. Clearly, the longer the period the greater the risk that the credit worthiness of the counterparty may deteriorate.

- *Daily settlement limits*: As noted above, this has been partially addressed but is still a major issue given the enormous daily volumes now traded. Similarly, daylight limits (overdrafts) are imposed by correspondent banks. This will limit the number of payments made during the day without cover. There will be limits as to the amount of money that can be left overnight in nostro accounts.

- *Specific limits*: Individual limits will be established for each counterparty and for each country.

- *Individual limit*: A chief dealer or treasurer may be given specific limits to approve a particular trade.

- *Loss limits*: There may be limits on individual traders' losses or how much the desk can lose. This will be enforced by stop loss orders placed in the market.

MONITORING FORWARD FOREIGN EXCHANGE EXPOSURE

Original exposure methodology

Under original exposure methodology (OEM) the gross limit is used to control the amount of foreign exchange transactions the counterparty may have outstanding with the bank at any one time. The risk being protected against is that the client may default before the settlement date and that the bank as a result would have to replace the transaction. In such a case, exchange rates may have moved adversely and the bank may incur a loss. The bank therefore has to make a credit decision whatever the type of counterparty. For individuals and small corporates a margin – a percentage of the notional amount – may be required to cover this. The credit risk is measured only at the time of trade being executed, hence the name 'original exposure methodology'.

The weakness of OEM is that it does not measure the replacement cost over time as exchange rates actually move. In addition, it does not differentiate between the relative volatility of differing currency pairs or between transactions of differing maturities, say one month or one year. It also means that gross limits will have to be increased to cover rollovers and closing out trades as exposure will not be netted. As a result, OEM is now rarely used and the preferred methodology is mark-to-market.

Mark-to-market methodology

Mark-to-market methodology (MTM) is where each outstanding transaction is compared against the current day's spot rate and a replacement cost calculated as if the deal had to be replaced that day using that rate. If the trade is in the money the cost is set at zero. In some systems an allowance is also made for potential future currency movements based on option volatilities.

Value at risk (VAR)

This is the most common model that financial institutions employ to estimate risk exposures. Value at risk (VAR) models seek to quantify the expected maximum loss of a dealer (or bank) over a set time period (usually one day), within a certain confidence level, based on the historical performance of the assets involved. A 99% confidence level was widely used in the 1990s but it is now more common to see 95%. For instance, a 5% VAR of GBP 1m means that on 95% of days you will lose less than GBP 1m.

As we saw in the discussion on liquidity and the carry trade, it is a big ask for models to function in times of crisis. Thus VAR estimates cannot really tell how bad it may be in that last 1% to 5% of the time. In other words, these models cannot be relied on to predict outcomes in periods of crisis.

When volatility is low in the markets these models typically offer a very flattering picture of risk. This leads banks to take on more risk, which can reduce volatility further. If market volatility starts to turn, this process goes into sharp reverse. The easiest way to reduce risk exposure is to sell risky assets, but a problem occurs when everyone is trying to do the same. As a result, volatility rises and in turn VAR and efforts to reduce risk come to nothing.

In brief, the two main issues with VAR are that estimates are based on past data which may not be representative of the future and extreme outcomes are more likely than expected. VAR fails to take account of the likelihood of extreme events because it assumes a normal distribution of outcomes when in reality the markets are prone to fat tails (kurtosis) and skewness (the distribution is not symmetrical around the mean).

VAR does have appeal in so far as a number implies precision and is simple to monitor. It also has an appeal to management because it allows them to give a scientific basis to their risk-taking. It also allows them to explain to shareholders that losses are due to astonishing circumstances rather than taking large risks that were not understood.

14.

DEALING WITH BANKS AND FINANCIAL INSTITUTIONS

The importance of using the right counterparty cannot be overstated. Whether you are an individual or a company, large or small, the approach is broadly similar. A number of questions need to be addressed. This review would normally be made at the outset of a dealing relationship and thereafter on an annual basis.

THE PROVIDER SHOULD BE FINANCIALLY STRONG

Events of 2007-09 have highlighted the need for substantive research in this area. There have been very few instances of foreign exchange losses related to the failure of a bank or financial institution, but if a counterparty does have difficulties it will take up time better utilised elsewhere, apart from the unnecessary stress involved.

It is also important to evaluate the credit of the provider's country of origin and to ascertain whether the country has the resources to support banks and financial institutions in the last resort.

THE PROVIDER SHOULD BE OPERATIONALLY STRONG

It is one thing to execute a transaction, but it has to be settled correctly. A bank that gives the best rate in the market but then makes the payment late or to the wrong beneficiary is not the best bank to be dealing with. For individuals and companies such errors may damage reputations and lead to financial losses, which may not always be retrievable in full. Errors will inevitably occur but the time taken to identify errors and the speed at which they are corrected is a key indicator of a provider's operational abilities.

There are two further areas of importance here: confirmations and security. Confirmations need to be clear and produced quickly. There needs to be an accounting record, an audit trail, and confirmations should be checked to ensure that the trade is correct. There also need to be systems in place to ensure that the right people trade and in the amounts, maturities and products agreed. A dealing mandate needs to be agreed and signed off by the parties.

CHECK THE BANK CAN SUPPLY THE PRODUCT AND SERVICE YOU REQUIRE

It is important to have a clear idea of what you are trying to achieve. You can then work with the bank to establish the best solution. Talking in advance also gives you the opportunity to see if the foreign exchange provider can meet all or any of your requirements. This could be their range of currencies, options traded, maximum maturities, pricing spreads or the level of risk the bank is prepared to take on.

Banks will have different perceptions of risks and differing business propositions. For instance, some will focus on low margin and high volume while others will look for higher margins with less focus on volume. For large companies they will put high value on banks who will quote regardless of volatility and at the same time not materially widen the dealing spreads. As an example, if you only have a few trades a year of modest size to make a provider that is seeking high volume will give you great prices but will not have any interest in talking through these trades with you.

Virtually anyone can quote the major currencies and the pricing is very similar for normal market sizes. When it comes to emerging markets though – South American, African, East European and some Asian trading – it becomes more complicated. This can be due to onerous exchange control regulations or for example where there is no forward market and only non-deliverable forwards are available. This is where the specialists can add value. First, they can provide advice and second they can provide the best execution and settlement. Certainly not every foreign exchange provider can achieve this.

A further consideration is the ability to do trades in size. Market sizes will vary considerably between currencies and the ability of the bank to get the trade away without unduly spoiling the market is important. In other words, does the provider in question have an internal liquidity pool? This can also be critical when stop losses are involved as there is increased risk of being filled away from the order level if the bank is reliant on outside sources.

Allied to this is how dealing spreads react to differing market conditions or indeed whether the bank might even cease quoting in certain conditions. It is unrealistic to expect the same pricing for all conditions and conditions can vary a lot, which is not always obvious to the customer.

Increasingly, customers are dealing via electronic platforms. This is very convenient and gives you pricing access virtually all the time. The banks have spent millions on dealing technology and they want you to use it. The issue then is what kind of input you require from the dealers. If you wish to have direct contact it is best to establish on what basis this comes. If there is an advisory service, check whether it will be charged for or if it comes free and what products the service would apply to.

DEALING MANDATE

A treasury dealing mandate will establish who can deal, in what product, in what quantity of product, and where the funds can be paid to. In this context the company would provide a board resolution, and Memorandum and Articles of Association, to confirm dealing parameters. The message to take from this is that documentation, procedures and controls are all-important and should be established at the outset for all types of transactions.

FOREIGN EXCHANGE LIMITS

Before a corporate or individual can enter into a foreign exchange or option transaction it is normal for the bank to agree limits on this trading. Foreign exchange limits are not committed facilities as a rule, although the client is normally advised of them. In other words, the bank can decline to trade at any time if it wishes.

The bank will determine the total amount of contracts that can be outstanding and the maximum maturity allowed for any contract. For large corporates this is based on the strength of the company and no margin or collateral is usually required. For small and private companies and individuals the requirements can be quite demanding: margin requirements, floating or fixed charges or personal guarantees. As a general rule the longer the contract maturities the greater security required.

Limits are set up for forward and spot trades. The latter are sometimes viewed as riskless but when they are settled over external (nostro) accounts funds could still be paid away before receipt. Trades settled over internal accounts clearly attach minimal risk; in these cases funds are already in situ.

The last crucial point is to fully understand at the outset how the outstanding on a limit is calculated. Clearly what is outstanding will determine how many more trades and of what size can be executed. Is the methodology original exposure or mark-to-market, for instance? Are buy and sell trades netted out to calculate exposure? Clarification avoids turning down customers, and customers unable to execute a transaction which they thought they could.

UNDERSTANDING WHAT IS ON OFFER

Banks offer complex structures and there are usually fees imbedded within these apart from the headline cost. Simplicity is on many occasions the best option. Individuals and companies still enter into transactions which they do not fully understand and this is not always the fault of the bank as people will claim to understand simply in order not to lose face.

That may apply to their contacts with the bank but also internally within their organisation.

AGREEMENTS

Large companies will use a variant on the International Swap Dealers Association, Inc. Master Agreement (ISDA). I say 'variant' as the large companies are in a position to edit elements they find onerous such as cross default clauses. The focus, even in the short form agreements, is on termination/default and the process thereafter.

Not everyone uses an ISDA and an alternative is a simple netting agreement. Netting is also referred to in the Master Agreement and also the Treasury Dealing Mandate. Netting is clearly important in liquidation situations but it also can be important in everyday trading as to how it impacts on your dealing limit. For instance, if you buy GBP 1m and sell GBP 1m for the same day, all things being equal, the outstanding under the limit would be zero under a netting agreement or could be GBP 2m.

Any agreement should be left in the hands of your lawyers.

BANKS DEALING WITH CUSTOMERS

The most important mantra in banking is *understand your customer*. This is true for the individual as much as for the corporate.

The large companies in some cases know more than the banks. However, small to medium-sized companies and most individuals need assistance. The bank can play a major role in adding value by providing a hedging methodology as well as the tools to execute. The banker has the responsibility to identify or understand the foreign exchange risks of their client.

It is important to be transparent in pricing. Large companies and some individuals will have access to live pricing and others will not but, either way, whether the customer receives the straight interbank rate or if there is a margin involved, it is well to advise on your approach prior to dealing.

Managing client expectations is crucial. Do not promise what you cannot consistently deliver. This not only risks losing the relationship but also market reputation. It is also worthwhile dispelling the notion that profits are assured for every trade. This applies to both large and small trades. If you treat your customer fairly there should not be many contentious issues to deal with.

The bank should always adopt best practice in documentation and secure trading.

AFTERWORD

M arx alleged that history repeats itself, first as tragedy, then as farce. And Cordell Hull asserted in 1948 that "unhampered trade dovetailed with peace," and with "high tariffs… war".

These comments quite clearly were made some time ago, but I have in front of me a *Financial Times* dated 15 October 2010. The headline reads, "Tumble in dollar triggers warning of destabilising effect on global economy" and the attached article says "…and push other countries into retaliatory devaluations to support their exports".

You may well sense that economic management has not really progressed since the 1930s. I am ending this book as I started – with a deep unease about financial policies that create huge imbalances and in turn create huge volatility in exchange rates. While central bankers call for stability, decrying excessive moves as undesirable, there is little chance when monetary and fiscal policies are regularly out of step.

As I noted at the beginning of this book, to achieve stability politicians will have to learn to live with financial discipline and take responsibility for managing electoral expectations. The inevitable consequences of extreme exchange rate volatility are reduced trade and investment flows, lower growth and conflict.

Volatility, however, can be managed, which undoubtedly is the core of the book. I have also shown various methods that can be employed to reduce foreign exchange risk. This of course does not come cost-free and transactional costs of hedging need to be factored in. It is also the case that realistically hedging is only viable or practical for a limited period. In other words, sharp swings will catch you up in the end.

As I suggest, the fatal flaw in a floating exchange rate system is that overshoots and undershoots from long-run equilibrium values do occur, and for protracted periods of time. Some will argue of course that devaluation is a useful tool for easing the adjustment process. Greece and Ireland, and their economic problems in 2010 and 2011, are cited in this context. However, their problems come from financial indiscipline and debt rather than an overvalued exchange rate.

As I write I am increasingly concerned by the concentration of foreign exchange volumes within a handful of banks. This has been further accentuated, I believe, by the development of electronic dealing platforms that require enormous development costs and in turn create a barrier to entry for other banks. The daily reported foreign exchange turnover would suggest that there is enormous liquidity in the market and therefore there is obviously no issue. However, I suggest that this may be an illusion as this enormous liquidity pot is really only a handful of liquidity pools.

Of equal concern is the growth of computer-generated trading through these electronic portals. I have reservations that the market cannot always support the volume and size of trades associated with these models and that they will destabilise the market even in liquid currency pairs. Regulators will need to take a closer look at this type of dealing.

The foreign exchange markets though have come out of the 2007-09 financial crisis pretty well. Transactions and settlement continued in extreme conditions. Indeed, the crisis was little to do with the foreign exchange markets.

Nonetheless, the global financial turmoil has raised many questions about how much freedom financial markets should have in regulating themselves. The foreign exchange market is no exception and the inevitable focus going forward will be on derivatives/options and related structured products which have seen such rapid growth over the past 15 years.

The argument is that at least some of the accelerated moves in the foreign exchange market during the turmoil came from structured products. A BIS study into market volatility suggested that in periods of rising volatility these products can accentuate the price action and raise market volatility.[10] However, in more stabile periods the selling of derivatives leads to lower foreign exchange volatility. This is consistent with the notion that lower volatility leads to greater risk-taking (e.g., carry trades).

Legislation is likely to involve increased capital requirements and increased use of exchange clearing for derivatives, with a view to improving market transparency which will inevitably raise the cost. There is also of course the possibility of a currency transaction tax, or what is popularly known as *Robin*

---

[10] BIS Paper 29, 2006.

Hood or *Tobin* tax. For politicians and those with vested interests the prospect is mouth watering. Huge volumes and a very low tax equals colossal revenues. For some like Lord Turner, an advocate, he views it as a means to cutting the banks down to size. For others like Stamp Out Poverty, a network of charities, the money raised can be used to reduce poverty in poorer countries. As is usually the case the proponents of new taxes provide some ingenious, or from my viewpoint spurious, reasons for its adoption.

If you believe volatility is due to excessive speculation then the argument goes that raising the cost of dealing will reduce these highly speculative trades and in turn volatility. With this they also argue that it could help business with reduced hedging costs. Of course, if the initial tax does not work they can temporarily impose a higher tax rate, referred to as a 'circuit breaker'. They might as well then suggest fixed exchange rate systems and the required financial discipline that goes with it. It could, however, be argued that if a tax reduced activity it will also reduce liquidity in the market; and, in the catalogue of unintended consequences, this can perversely increase volatility.

It would be incorrect to suggest that speculation is not a factor in foreign exchange volatility. It is my view that it is not the cause of economic instability or mismanagement, it is a symptom. All governments, central banks and regulators post-crisis have done a remarkably good job in presenting the banks as the culprits but it is arguable whether speculators are really in control. There is a strong body of opinion that it is real money or portfolio flows and the variable hedging related to these investments that is the prime driver of currency markets. History indicates that it is institutional failure that ultimately undermines foreign exchange markets and in turn the financial system, not the dealer looking at a screen.

As you have come to end of this book you should have full command of all the jargon. Whether it be 'spot', 'forward', 'put' or 'call', you will have a knowledge of the construction of these trades and their significance.

Foreign exchange is simple but not easy to take on at the first attempt. In its raw state you either buy or sell, now or at a date in the future. Armed with this information you may wish to speculate. This is where volatility is your friend. I have provided a dealing template which will set you on the right course; it is not a guarantee of riches. There is no magic formula as the formula keeps changing. The carry trade, for instance, was a licence to print money until the licence was revoked. Technical analysis, model trading systems, forecasts do work, but not all the time. There is no evidence that one system consistently works and beware of performance claims.

I have devoted some time to the psychology of trading. It is not just about understanding numbers, important as they are. It is about understanding ourselves and to some extent other participants. Behavioural science offers a great deal in our understanding of decision making under pressure and further reading in this area is recommend.

This book also acknowledges that our approach and capacity for risk will vary. For individuals and even corporates the first step is to identify the risk. From here the most suitable solution can be selected. I have shown that corporates and individuals can look to protect their margins/profits and their business through relatively simple processes.

In every trade there is a counterparty, which for companies and individuals will normally be a bank. In this context I highlighted the importance of selecting the right counterparty and listed the most important considerations to make this decision. It is important that this is set up correctly from the outset to meet your current needs and possible future requirements.

Lastly, the issue of transaction costs is not as critical in foreign exchange as in other asset classes as pricing for most is at or very close to interbank levels. It is nonetheless a consideration if very active trading is envisaged or practised. What is more important is the understanding between risk and return, price and value. What price do you put on certainty?

I conclude where I started. I am afraid that history since 1918 suggests that foreign exchange stability is a distant dream and volatility is the natural state in a dislocated world order. There will be an ongoing need to manage foreign exchange risk. With that in mind this book looks set to have an enduring relevance.

APPENDICES

APPENDIX 1.
FOREIGN EXCHANGE SOLUTIONS IN BRIEF

Example 1

Customer wishes to buy a Spanish villa with cash.

- Now: use a spot trade, short-term considerations.
- In six months: use a forward trade, medium-term considerations, forecasts, current spot price, interest rate differentials.
- Customer borrows in a low interest rate currency and converts: use a spot trade, which gives a gain on interest cost but some spot risk. This is a carry trade.

Example 2

Customer wishes to fund Spanish property with sterling cash but wants no exchange rate risk: use an FX swap. There is interest rate risk.

Example 3

Customer has already bought property but will return to UK: sell EUR forward and use a rolling hedge (FX swap). This protects proceeds.

Example 4

Customer funds property in local currency = No FX risk.

Example 5

UK customer invests in overseas fund, e.g., US.

- Option 1: Sell GBP for USD spot. This creates currency risk.
- Option 2: FX swap and create a perfect hedge. This will result in no currency risk, but there will be interest rate risk.

Example 6

Customer invested in US equity portfolio but worried about USD weakening but still wants to keep portfolio.

- Sell USD for future date with a forward trade. There is no spot risk.

- At future date, roll contract with an FX swap. There is interest rate risk.

APPENDIX 2.
A SIMPLE GUIDE TO TECHNICAL ANALYSIS

Introduction

I would like to cover the basic concepts of technical analysis and some of the commonly used jargon in this subject area. The objective of technical analysis is making an observation and translating it into a tradable solution.

Support and resistance

The most talked about concepts in technical analysis are *support* and *resistance*. Prominent peaks and troughs normally are the simple visual clues; an example of how these look is shown in Figure A1.

Figure A1 – Example of peaks and troughs on a price chart, showing support and resistance

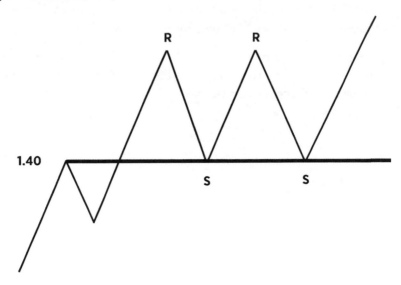

Market bought when the old high (resistance) at 1.4 was breached. Note the old resistance now becomes the support (and vice versa). This is referred to as polarity.

The difficulty is determining the importance one should attach to these support and resistance levels, and working out whether the trend is set to continue or whether the trend has reversed. The technical analyst will typically measure distances of moves from low to high, or high to low, and ratios of that distance to determine targets and support and resistance points in the future.

To calculate the likely retracement levels, i.e., how far the currency may retreat from a recently made high, the most common method is to employ Fibonacci retracement levels.

Fibonacci retracement levels

A mathematician called Leonardo Pisano introduced Fibonacci retracement levels in 1202 AD in his book *Liber Abacci*. He introduced the following series of numbers:

1, 1, 2, 3, 5, 8, 13, 21, 34, 55, 89, etc.

If we take the ratio of two successive numbers in the series ($1/1 = 1$, $2/1 = 2$, $3/2 = 1.5$, $5/3 = 1.6$, $8/5 = 1.6$, $13/8 = 1.625$, $21/13 = 1.61538$, $34/21 = 1.619048$, $55/34 = 1.617647$, $89/55 = 1.618182$, etc.) the ratio gradually moves towards approximately 1.618034, which is called the *golden ratio* or the *golden number*.

This golden ratio is used by analysts as the key level to determine whether the trend is corrective or a reversal. Exceeding 61.8% of the move is viewed as a major break. Other common ratios applied to charts are 0.236%, 0.382%, 0.5% and 0.764%.

Chart patterns

Chart patterns are divided into two groups:

1. Reversal patterns
2. Continuation patterns

1. Reversal patterns

There are a number of elements to note in reversal patterns. First, intuitively, there has to be a prior trend and the longer the pattern the more significant it is. Second, an important trend line or support/resistance has to be breached. Volume is important in technical analysis but in foreign exchange this is not available (apart from for exchange-traded contracts).

Head and shoulders

A head and shoulders pattern is characterised by ascending peaks and troughs and the failure of the return move to take out the neckline. The pattern is illustrated in Figure A2.

Figure A2 – Example head and shoulders pattern

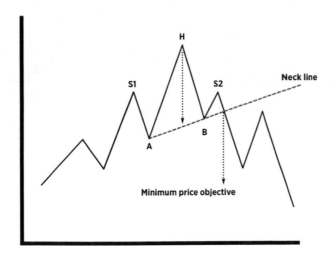

This could be a five-year uptrend so the reversal should be aggressive. Some analysts would prefer to see two closes below the neckline for confirmation. Ideally, S2 should be below S1, and B should be above A.

Note that the return move fails to take out the neckline and in this case this is the sell trigger. Traders always look for head and shoulders patterns as the success rate is very high.

Figure A3 shows a particularly spectacular example in GBP/JPY. It all seems so obvious now.

Figure A3 – A head and shoulders example from GBP/JPY

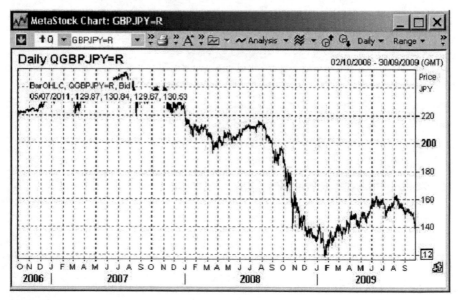

Source: Reuters

Inverse head and shoulders

For an inverse head and shoulders pattern the analyst would look for three distinct bottoms and a close above the neckline. A downward sloping neckline is preferred. The pattern is illustrated in Figure A4.

Figure A4 – An inverse head and shoulders pattern

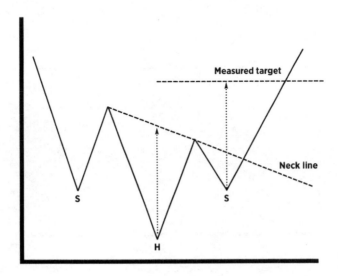

Double top (M top)

In a double top pattern the two tops are at the same level and the trigger point is the mid-point A. Timing between the peaks is considered important and traders like to see at least a one-month gap. An illustration of a double top pattern is given in Figure A5.

Figure A5 – A double top pattern

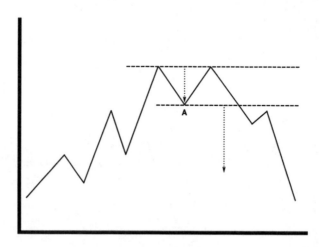

Figure A6 is a very good example of a double top reversal pattern in EUR/USD from 2008.

Figure A6 – An example of a double top reversal from EUR/USD

Source: Reuters

Double bottom (W bottom)

A double bottom looks like the letter W. It will include a low that has been touched twice – this low is then regarded as a support level. Figure A7 provides an illustration of a double bottom pattern.

Figure A7 – A double bottom pattern

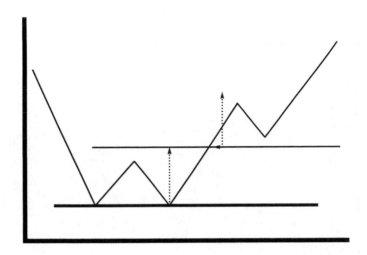

2. Continuation patterns

A continuation pattern occurs when a price trend exhibits a temporary diversion from its previous behaviour, and indicates that the existing trend will eventually continue.

Triangles

Symmetrical triangle

In a symmetrical triangle pattern there are four reversal points and two converging trend lines. The breakout target is the height of the triangle. The breakout should be about halfway or two-thirds of the way into the pattern. Figure A8 provides an illustration of a symmetrical triangle.

Figure A8 – A symmetrical triangle pattern

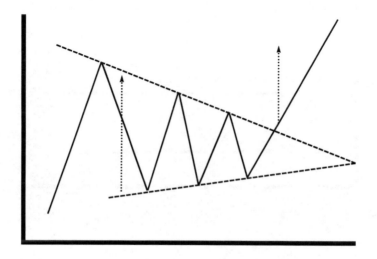

Expanding triangle

In an expanding triangle the breakout is seen when the rejection from the third peak (trough) violates support (resistance). Failure to retest the upper (lower) boundary could be a clue to the breakout. Figures A9 and A10 give illustrations of this pattern and an example of it from a EUR/GBP price chart where the failure to retest the lower boundary line proved to be crucial.

Figure A9 – An expanding triangle pattern

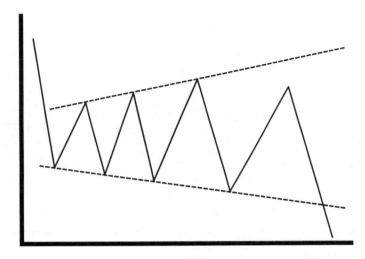

Figure A10 – An expanding triangle seen in EUR/GBP

Ascending triangle

With an ascending triangle the breakout should be halfway or two-thirds of the way along the triangle. The upper line is horizontal (breakout side) and the lower line is upward sloping. Figure A11 provides an illustration of an ascending triangle.

Figure A11 – An ascending triangle pattern

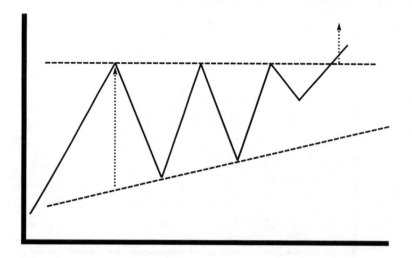

Flags and pennants

Bull flag

A bull flag is normally a short-term pattern and is set against a steep price trend. The flags are said to fly at half-mast, contained within a sloping parallelogram. The price objective is therefore aggressive.

This and similar patterns are not easy to trade as it appears you are trading against the trend. Figure A12 provides an illustration of a bull flag.

Figure A12 – A bull flag pattern

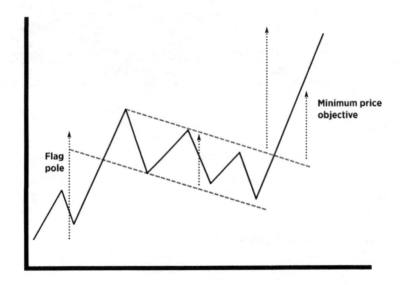

The bear flag is simply the opposite pattern to a bull flag, continuing a bear trend.

Figure A13 shows a good example of a bearish flag in EUR/USD.

Figure A13 – A bear flag in EUR/USD

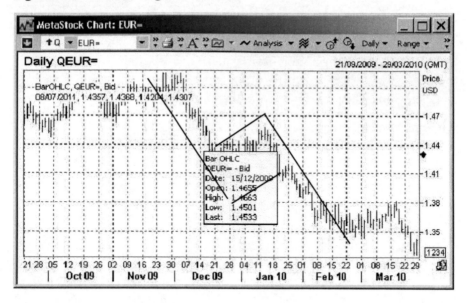

Bullish pennant

A bullish pennant pattern is generally short term, one to two weeks, and is similar to a symmetrical triangle with a minimum price target the height of the lines. An illustration of a bullish pennant is given in Figure A14.

Figure A14 – A bullish pennant

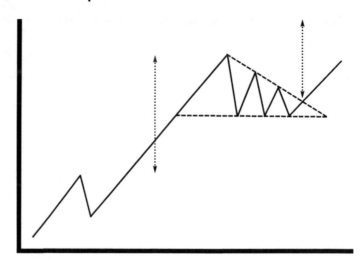

Wedges

A wedge is composed of two converging lines that connect a series of highs and lows in price. This pattern usually occurs for one to three months maximum. Wedges are difficult to trade simply because they are against current price action.

A breakout from the wedge is either bullish or bearish, depending on its direction. The break is usually halfway or two-thirds of the way to the apex.

Bullish wedge

A bullish wedge is an interruption of a rising price trend. It is illustrated in Figure A15.

Figure A15 – A bullish wedge

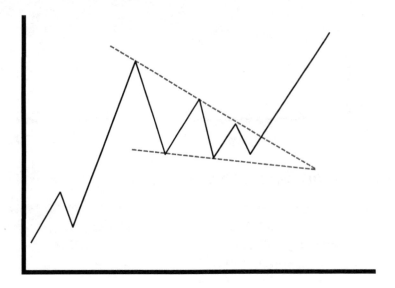

Bearish wedge

A bearish wedge is the same as a bullish wedge but is the interruption of a falling price trend. The bearish wedge is similar to the symmetrical triangle but the difference is that both lines are sloping away from the prevailing trend. An illustration of the bearish wedge is given in A16.

Figure A16 – A bearish wedge

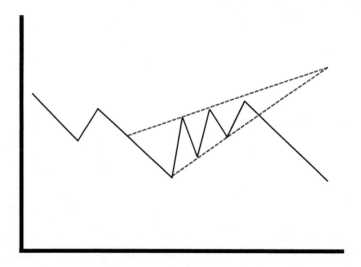

Simple trend lines and channels

A trend line measures the gradient of the price and can be upward sloping, downward sloping or flat. A break of a trend line confirms that the trend is no longer continuing at the same pace, which can be the first indication of a turn or a pause. However, if the original trend was very steep a break may just indicate a return to a more usual gradient.

Support lines are drawn from the lows in an uptrend while resistance lines are drawn from the highs in a downtrend. Intuitively, one can see that the more often a trend line is tested and holds the stronger it becomes. It is desirable that there are at least three points of contact to draw a trend line (two is insufficient). Trend lines should capture most of the price action but not necessarily all of it. More importantly, prices should react at the lines.

There are a number of methods to validate a trend line break; these include two consecutive closes above the line, a weekly close above the line, and an entire day's trading above the line. Figure A17 provides a diagram to illustrate lines and channels.

Figure A17 – Trend lines and a channel

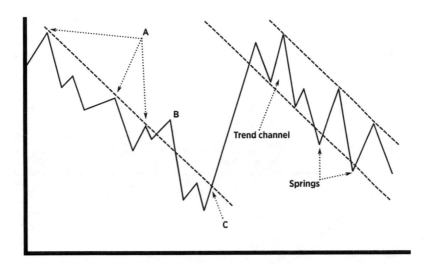

In Figure A17, multiple points (A) of contact will suggest a better trend line. B was a false break but the trend line finally is breached at C. To create the trend line channel in a downtrend, draw a resistance line first and then draw a parallel line off the lows. In an uptrend, draw a support line first and then a parallel resistance line. It is important to monitor the reaction at the trend line for direction clues.

The angle of the channel is important as steeper ones break quicker. Always try to leave the trend lines on the chart and extend them. The same principal applies to a neck line on a head and shoulders pattern.

Figure A18 shows a channel drawn onto a price chart of GBP/JPY.

Figure A18 – A channel drawn onto a GBP/JPY price chart

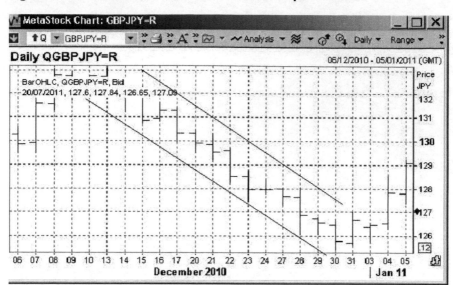

Key period reversals – outside days

A bullish outside day is when you see a lower low, higher high, and a higher close than the previous session. A bearish outside day is when you see a higher high, lower low and a close lower than the previous session. If these occur after strong counter-trend moves it may be the first sign of a change in the trend. These are more obvious on monthly charts. Similarly, weekly rather than daily charts provide a clearer picture. Figure A19 provides an illustration of a bullish outside day situation.

Figure A19 – A bullish outside day

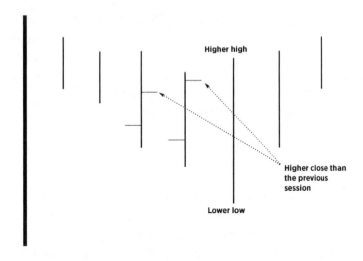

Gaps

Gaps are formed on daily bar charts where no trading has taken place. In an upside gap a gap would be formed if the open is higher than the previous bar's high. A downside gap would be formed if the open was lower than the previous bar's low.

These gapping moves form true gaps when at the end of the trading day the gap is left unfilled. So in an upside gap today's low is higher than the previous bar's high; in a downside gap today's high is lower than the previous bar's low.

There is a common belief that gaps must be filled but this is not always true. The gap does, however, grow in significance if it is left unfilled. This price behaviour in itself offers little in terms of trend breakout or reversal analysis. However, the gap high and low and the close and open are frequently used as support and resistance levels. This has importance in so far as orders are left to cut losses or initiate trades. Indeed, prices can leap as these orders are triggered creating what is referred to as *breakaway* or *runaway* gaps which do give a strong signal that a new trend or phase of a trend has started.

Moving averages

Moving averages can be used to refine a technical analysis approach. They are an entirely objective technique in so far as the outcome is derived from a mathematical calculation. Moving averages are used to smooth out price movements. The idea is to eliminate short-term volatility (noise) that could distort the overall trend. Moving averages are therefore very useful in determining the trend and can provide support and resistance levels. Thus, moving averages can be used as a directional tool, providing signals. For example, if the price is below the short-term moving average it suggests that the short-term trend is positive.

One can use a combination of moving averages of different time frames to give trend and directional guidance. The usual approach is to see if the short-term moving averages are crossing the longer-term averages. If so this is considered a bullish crossover. If the longer-term average is above the short-term average this is referred to as a 'bearish crossover'.

A favoured directional indicator is when a triple crossover occurs. This is when three moving averages – short term, medium term and long term – cross. An example of this is called the *dead cross* when a five-day moving average crosses a 20-day moving average and a 20-day moving average crosses a 60-day moving average all on the same day.

Another example of a triple crossover is referred to as the *golden cross*. This is when the 20-day moving average crosses the 60-day moving average and the 60-day moving average crosses the 200-day moving average.

Types of moving average

Simple

To calculate a simple moving average for n days add up the last n prices and divide by n. The same weight is given to each price; in other words, we treat the most recent price exactly the same to an old price. If n = 6, and P6 is the most recent price:

simple moving average = (P1+P2+P3+P4+P5+P6)/6

Linear weighted

A linear weighted moving average is more refined than the plain simple moving average as it gives greater weight to the more recent prices. Again only the prices in the period covered are taken into account. The moving average is normally plotted at the end of the period covered. For a series of six prices the calculation of the linear weighted moving average would be as follows:

weighted moving average = (P1+(P2*2)+(P3*3)+(P4*4)+ P5*5)+(P6*6))/6

Exponential

To find the exponential moving average for n days:

exponential moving average = (today's price − yesterday's moving average) x 2/(n+1)

2/n+1 is called the exponential constant.

All previous prices are taken into account in the calculation of this average. Greater weight is given to the more recent prices, discounting older values in an exponential manner.

Summary

Moving averages are a useful addition to traditional charting analysis. They nevertheless have some inherent flaws, not least because they are a lagging indicator which will inevitably miss part of the move. It also tends to work better in a trending market and not particularly well in sideways trading. Its influence on trading patterns, however can be greater than at first sight as many model trading programmes use moving averages in the trading programmes. The simple moving average will do the job for the vast majority of applications.

Momentum

You will regularly hear expressions such as *overbought, oversold, overcooked* and *running out of steam*. These refer to momentum. Momentum measures the speed of the change in prices. The analyst is looking at the rate of ascent or decent by plotting price differences for a set period of time. Momentum is calculated as follows:

Momentum = V - Vx

Where:

V = latest closing price

Vx is the close x days ago

A positive figure shows that momentum is rising and a negative number indicates that momentum is falling. If prices are rising and the momentum line, when plotted, is also rising, that shows that the uptrend is accelerating. If the momentum trend line has flattened out this means that the rates of gain are the same.

When momentum begins to decline the uptrend may still be in place but will be at a decelerating pace: the uptrend is losing momentum. Momentum then leads price action, whether it be a decline or an advance, and levels off while the current price trend is still in effect. It then begins to move in the opposite direction as prices begin to level off. Momentum indicators will provide clues as to trend direction, although it is felt that they are more reliable at the end of a market move rather than at the beginning of important moves.

Momentum tools are used to signal whether the market is in overbought or oversold territory. This occurs when the market has been trending in a relatively steep fashion for some time. This concept has its roots in positioning. This is where those who have bought or sold dominate and have come to the limit of their appetite to take it further. In other words, there are fewer participants to jump on the band wagon. These type of conditions can prompt a correction, although you should bear in mind even if momentum is at an extreme level it is not necessarily a signal for a trend reversal. Nonetheless, for short-term trading it is a useful indicator.

A useful signal to the analyst is when prices continue to trend up or down and the momentum indicator is travelling in the opposite direction. This is referred to as bullish or bearish divergence. Under bullish (positive) divergence, prices in a declining trend make lower lows but momentum does not follow (known as failure swing), and under bearish (negative) divergence prices make ascending highs in a rising trend and momentum has decreasing highs. This is a sign that while the trend is still intact as evidenced by the move to a new high or low, the speed of the rise or fall is falling.

Relative Strength Index (RSI)

The Relative Strength Index compares the average gain on the days with positive closes with the average loss on the days with a negative close, over a chosen time period. This is expressed as a number from 0 to 100. Generally, a 14-day period is used, but this can be adjusted depending on the volatility of the market. The 14-day RSI is calculated as:

RSI = 100-(100/(1+RS))

Where:

RS = average of the past 14 positive closes/average of the past 14 negative closes

Note that only changes in closing prices are used.

The market is viewed as oversold if the RSI dips through 30 and viewed as overbought if 70 is broken, although in strongly trending markets 20 and 80 may be used. The RSI is usually plotted below the price chart to provide easy comparison with the price action.

A word of caution in using momentum indicators:

Any strong trend will inevitably throw up some high readings and this is not necessarily a good enough reason to close out a position. The key interest will be how the price reacts to these levels. At least you will be aware of what the market is looking at.

Markets, however, can stay in overbought or oversold territory for some period of time. In this situation it is good to reflect why a particular currency was weak or strong in the first place and what might have changed to dilute that. In the end it is just as well to picture an elastic band that is being stretched.

Moving average convergence/divergence (MACD)

This indicator comes highly recommended. A refinement to using moving averages is to use the difference between two exponential moving averages, revolving above and below a zero line, with crossovers in the averages triggering buy/sell signals.

The moving average convergence/divergence (MACD) uses two exponential moving averages of differing time periods. A buy signal occurs when the shorter line crosses above the longer, and a sell when it crosses below the longer line. In other words, a cross above zero generates a buy signal while a cross below zero is a sell signal. As the MACD moves towards 0 (convergence of the two exponential averages) it indicates trend termination or consolidation.

One of the advantages of using a MACD is that it further helps to identify overbought or oversold levels, which indicates when a short-term trend is overextended relative to its longer-term trend. The trouble for waiting for the multiple crossover is that you will probably miss most of the move.

Bollinger Bands

Bollinger Bands consist of a middle band with two outer bands. The middle band is a simple 20-day moving average. The outer bands are usually set two standard deviations above and below the middle band. Bands are calculated using closing prices and therefore signals should also be based on closing prices.

The purpose of Bollinger Bands is to provide a relative definition of high and low. Moves above or below the bands are not signals per se. As John Bollinger puts it, moves that touch or exceed the bands are not signals, but rather tags. On the face of it, a move to the upper band shows strength, while a sharp move to the lower band shows weakness.

Momentum oscillators work much the same way. They are used to determine if prices are relatively high or low. According to Bollinger, the bands should normally contain 95% of price action (typically less) which makes moves outside the bands significant. They are not viewed as a standalone tool and should be combined with other indicators (e.g., RSI).

The use of Bollinger Bands varies widely among traders. Some traders buy when price touches the lower Bollinger Band and exit when price touches the moving average in the centre of the bands. You can see in Figure A20 that in an upward trend the average acts as support and in a downward trend the average acts as resistance.

Traders also sell options when Bollinger Bands are historically far apart or buy options when the Bollinger Bands are historically close together, in both instances expecting volatility to revert back towards the average historical volatility level. When the bands lie close together a period of low volatility is indicated. Narrowing of the bands is typically a precursor to trending moves.

Figure A20 shows an example of Bollinger Bands on a GBP/CHF chart.

Figure A20 – Bollinger Bands drawn onto a GBP/CHF chart

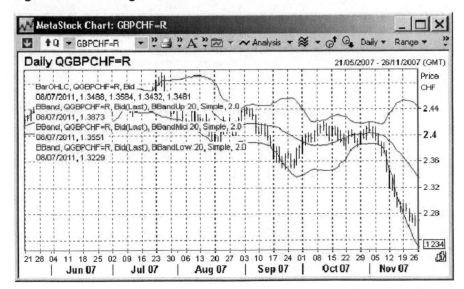

When the bands are far apart, a period of high volatility in price is indicated. When the bands have only a slight slope and lie approximately parallel for an extended time the price will be found to oscillate up and down between the bands as though in a channel. Price can, and does, walk up the upper Bollinger Band and down the lower Bollinger Band. Closes outside the Bollinger Bands can be continuation signals, not reversal signals.[11]

---

[11] John Bollinger, *Bollinger on Bollinger Bands* (McGraw Hill, 2002).

Final thoughts on momentum

Momentum indicators are not a substitute for trend analysis. It is important to recognise that the trend dominates and beware of contra-trades built on these indicators. Divergence analysis is extremely useful and these indicators can assist in timing market entry. In a sideways trading market, divergence indicators can be very useful for range trading.

Technical trading

The holy grail of dealing is to get on the right end of a trend. If technical analysis is potentially a key part of that process then it is difficult to ignore. A constant message in technical analysis is to wait for breakouts rather than try to anticipate them. This raises a number of issues, one of which is a tendency to look for multiple confirmations which, if followed, can result in missing a large degree of the move. The use of momentum/divergence signals such as MACD can help in this regard.

Knowledge of technical support and resistance levels can be particularly useful in range trading markets, especially after there has been a major clearout of positions. They are also important in placing stop loss or take profit orders. I think the main danger is manipulating the chart to fit what one wants to see. Discipline applies to all forms of trading.

For the portfolio manager they cannot continually adjust their long-term currency asset allocation on the back of short-term technical signals. They will be mindful of potential major trend changes though. This is where the currency overlay manger will get involved using a combination of short-term currency trading strategies and fundamental economic analysis (fair value models) for longer-term core allocations.

GLOSSARY

American option An option that can be exercised at any time prior to and including the expiry date of the option.

Appreciation An increase in the value of a currency.

Arbitrage Dealing simultaneously in two markets to take advantage of temporary price distortions.

Ask/Offer The price the dealer will sell at; the price the buyer can buy at.

At the money An option whose strike price is equal to the price of the underlying instrument.

Base currency The currency that the customer buys or sells (i.e., EUR in EUR/USD, GBP in GBP/USD, and USD in USD/CHF).

Bear Someone who believes that price(s) are heading lower.

Bear squeeze Market pressure to force a bear to reduce the exchange exposure.

Bear spread Option strategy where spot rate is expected to fall but not strongly. It is achieved by buying a put at one strike price and selling a put at a lower strike price.

Betty Betty Grable/Cable. Rhyming slang for GBP/USD.

Bid The price the dealer will buy at.

Bid currency The currency being bought; the opposite is the **offer currency**.

Bid rate The bid rate is the rate at which you can sell.

Bull Someone who expects the price(s) to rise.

Bull spread Option strategy where the spot rate is expected to rise moderately; it is used where a strong positive result is not expected by just buying a call at one strike price and selling a call at a higher strike price.

Business day A day on which the transaction can be settled. In foreign exchange the two centres of the currencies dealt must be open.

Cable   GBP/USD.

Call   An option to buy.

Confirmation   The written contract note sent to confirm transaction details.

Convertible currency   A currency which can, without restriction, be exchanged into another.

Counterparty   The other party (bank, corporate, individual) involved in any transaction.

Credit limit   A limit established by a bank as to the maximum amount of business which it wishes to have outstanding with any one counterparty.

Cross   When trading with currencies, the investor buys one currency with another. These two currencies form the cross: for example, EUR/USD.

Cross rate   An exchange rate that is calculated from two other exchange rates. e.g., GBP/JPY.

Currency exposure   The sensitivity of an asset return, measured in the investor's domestic currency, to a movement in the exchange rate.

Currency overlay   The delegation of the management of currency risk in a portfolio to a currency specialist.

Delta   The rate of change of an option premium with respect to the underlying contract.

Depreciation/Decline   A fall in the value of a currency.

Devaluation   An official downward adjustment of a currency against its fixed parity.

Electronic communication networks (ECNs)   Computer-driven order system.

Equilibrium exchange rate   The rate at which demand for and supply of a currency are equal.

European option   An option that can be exercised only on the expiry date.

Exchange rate   The price at which one currency can be bought or sold and another purchased; what one currency is worth in terms of another.

Exchange rate systems   Countries can determine their exchange rates in a variety of ways:

1. A floating exchange rate system, where the currency finds its own level in the market.

2. A crawling or flexible peg system, which is a combination of an officially fixed rate and frequent small adjustments. This in theory works against a build-up of speculation about a revaluation or devaluation.

3. A fixed exchange rate system, where the value of the currency is set by the government and/or the central bank (this rate is called 'official parity'). Only limited fluctuations are allowed.

Exercise price   The rate at which an option may be exercised (strike rate).

Expiry date   The final date on which an option may be exercised.

Fixing   The market price at a particular time in the day, used for benchmarking. Notable times used are 11.00 am, 1.15 pm and 4.00 pm.

Foreign exchange   The conversion of one currency into another.

Forex   Foreign exchange, FX.

Forward points   Calculated from interest rate differentials between two currencies. These are added to or subtracted from the spot rate to give the forward rate.

Forward rate   The rate at which a foreign exchange contract is struck for a settlement beyond the spot date.

FX   Foreign exchange, Forex.

Gamma   The rate of change of an option premium with respect to delta.

Hedging   The limitation of risk. A tactic to offset a loss or a potential loss.

In the money   An option whose strike price is better than the current market price of the underlying instrument.

Interbank price   The price banks will trade with one another. Usually the finest price available. Sometimes referred to as wholesale price as compared to retail.

Interest rate differential   The yield spread between two otherwise comparable debt instruments denominated in different currencies.

Interest rate parity   This states that the interest rate differential between two countries equals the forward discount/premium through arbitrage.

Intrinsic value   The value of an option if it were exercised now; the difference between the strike price and the underlying instrument.

Leverage (gearing)   The investor only funds part of the amount traded; when a trader uses leverage they use borrowed capital to make a trade, with the expectation that their return will be greater than the amount borrowed and the cost of borrowing.

Long   To buy, usually with a view to selling it at a higher price.

Long position   A position that increases its value if market prices increase.

Liquid(-ity)   The capacity to be converted easily and with minimum loss. A liquid market is one in which there is enough activity to satisfy both buyers and sellers.

Margin   The deposit required when entering into a position as well as to hold an open position.

Maturity date   The settlement date for an exchange or option contract.

Nostro   A bank account held in a foreign country by a domestic bank, denominated in the currency of that country. Nostro accounts are used for the settlement of foreign exchange.

Offer currency   The currency being sold; opposite of the **bid currency**.

Open position   A position in a currency that has not yet been offset. For example, if you have bought in GBP/USD GBP 1m you have an open position in GBP/USD until you offset it by selling GBP/USD, thus closing the position.

Order (limit)   An order placed by a customer with a bank or by a bank with another bank to execute a foreign exchange contract at an agreed rate.

Over the counter   When trading takes place directly between two parties, rather than on an exchange. Over-the-counter trades can be customised whereas exchange-traded products are often standardised.

Out of the money   An option whose strike price is worse than the current market price of the underlying instrument.

Outright   A forward purchase or sale of a currency.

Pips   A pip is the smallest unit by which a Forex cross price quote changes. So if EUR/USD bid is now quoted at 1.2510 and it moves up 2 pips, it will be quoted at 1.2512.

Position   Traders talk of taking a position. This is the net overbought or oversold exposure in a currency pair.

Purchasing Power Parity (Absolute)   Absolute PPP between any two countries suggests that an amount of the currency of one country should enable the holder to buy the same amount of goods and services as would a stated amount of the currency of another country, if the exchange rate of one currency for the other currency is taken into account.

In reality it does not always work this way and so the **equilibrium exchange rate** is used to equalise the prices of a basket of goods between the two countries.

Purchasing Power Parity (Relative)   A refinement on absolute PPP that takes account of differences in inflation rates between countries. This is called relative PPP and states that changes in exchange rates should offset any inflation differential based on a basket of goods and services between the countries in question.

Put   An option to sell.

Rho   The sensitivity of the value of an option with respect to a change in the risk-free interest rate

Risk management   Trying to control outcomes to a known or predictable range of gains or losses. It involves several steps which begin with a sound understanding of one's business and the exposures or risks that have to be covered to protect the value of that business. Then an assessment should be made of the types of variables that can affect the business and how best to protect against unwelcome outcomes. Consideration must also be given to the preferred risk profile – whether one is risk-averse or fairly aggressive in approach. This also involves deciding which instruments to use to manage risk and whether a natural hedge exists that can be used. Once undertaken, a risk-management strategy should be continually assessed for effectiveness and cost.

Secondary currency (variable currency or counter currency)   The currency that the investor trades the base currency against (i.e., USD in EUR/USD, JPY in USD/JPY).

Short   To sell.

Short position   A position that benefits from a decline in market prices.

Speculative   Buying and selling in the hope of making a profit, rather than doing so for some fundamental business-related need.

Spot   The current market price of a currency pair.

Spot market   The part of the market calling for spot settlement of transactions. In the foreign exchange markets, 'spot' means delivery two working days hence.

Spread   The difference between the bid and the ask rate.

Strike rate or price   The rate at which an option may be exercised (exercise price).

Stop loss   An order to buy/sell at a rate worse than currently prevailing.

Swap   The initial exchange of currencies (usually spot) and the simultaneous reversal at some future date.

Theta   The rate of exchange of an option premium with respect to time.

Translation exposure (accounting exposure)   Measures the effect of an exchange rate change on the financial statements of a company.

Two-way price   A quotation which gives the buying and selling prices together.

Uncovered interest rate parity   Asserts that the expected change in the exchange rate is approximately equal to the interest rate differential between the two currencies.

Value date   The settlement date for an exchange contract.

Vega   The rate of change of an option premium with respect to volatility.

Volatility   A measure of price fluctuations.

Writer   The seller of an option.

BIBLIOGRAPHY

An, Lian and Sun, Wei, 'Monetary policy, Foreign Exchange Intervention, and the Exchange Rate: The Case of Japan', *International Journal of Finance and Economics* 15 (2008)

Bank for International Settlements, 'BIS Triennial central bank Survey' (2010)

Board of Governors of the Federal Reserve System, **www.federalreserve.gov**

Anderton, Alain, *Economics* (Causeway Press Ltd, 2000)

Ashley, Gerald, *Financial Speculation* (Harriman House, 2009)

Bergsten, C., 'Peterson Institute for International Economics', *Foreign Affairs* 88:6 (November/December 2009)

Bollinger, John, *Bollinger on Bollinger Bands* (McGraw Hill, 2002)

Dominguez, Kathryn and Frankel, Jeffrey, 'Does Foreign Exchange Intervention Work?', Washington, D.C. Institute for International Economics (1993)

Dominguez, Kathryn., 'Central bank intervention and exchange rate volatility', *Journal of International Money and Finance* 17 (1998)

Dornbusch, Rudiger, 'Expectations and Exchange Rate Dynamics', *Journal of Political Economy* 84:6 (1976)

Eichenbaum, Martin and Evans, Charles, 'Some empirical evidence on the effects of monetary policy shocks on exchange rates,' *Quarterly Journal of Economics* 110:4 (1995)

Euromoney, 'Euromoney FX Survey 2010'

Fatum, Rasmus, 'On the effectiveness of sterilised foreign exchange intervention', European Central Bank Working Paper Series (February 2000)

Fatum, Rasmus and Hutchison, Michael, 'Is Foreign Exchange Market Intervention an Alternative to Monetary Policy? Evidence from Japan', Danish National Research Foundation (2002)

Galati, Gabriele and Mellick, Will, 'Central Bank Intervention and Market Expectations', Bank for International Settlements Papers 10 (2002)

Kaminsky, Graciela and Lewis, Karen, 'Does Foreign Exchange Intervention Signal Future Monetary Policy?', *Journal of Monetary Economics* 37:2-3 (1996)

Galbraith, John. K., *Money, Whence It Came, Where It Went* (Penguin Books, 1975)

Gilovich, Thomas, Vallone, Robert and Tversky, Amos, 'The Hot Hand in Basketball: On the Misperception of Random Sequences', *Cognitive Psychology* 17 (1985)

Kahneman, Daniel and Riepe, Mark, 'Aspects of Investor Psychology', *Journal of Portfolio Management* 24:4 (1998)

Kim, Soyoung, 'Monetary policy, foreign exchange intervention, and the exchange rate in a unifying framework', *Journal of International Economics* 60:2 (2003)

Kindleberger, Charles, *Manias, Panics and Crashes: A History of Financial Crises* (J. Wiley & Sons, 1996)

Lewis, Karen, 'Are Foreign Exchange Intervention and Monetary Policy Related and Does It Really Matter?', *Journal of Business* 68:2 (1995)

Mainelli, Michael, 'Liquidity: Finance in motion or evaporation', Gresham College Lecture (5 September 2007)

Neely, Christopher J., 'The Practice of Central Bank Intervention: Looking Under the Hood', Federal Reserve Bank of St Louis (2001)

O'Hara, Maureen, 'Liquidity and Financial Market Stability', National Bank of Belgium Working Paper 55 (2004)

Persaud, Avinash, *Liquidity Black Holes: Understanding, Quantifying and Managing Financial Liquidity Risk* (Incisive RWG Ltd, 2003)

Rogoff, Kenneth, 'Dornbusch's Overshooting Model After Twenty-Five Years', Second Annual IMF Research Conference, Mundell-Fleming Lecture (2001)

Taylor, John, 'Lessons from the recovery from the "Lost Decade" in Japan: The Case of the Great Intervention and Money Injection', Stanford University, Background paper for the International Conference of the Economic and Social Research Institute Cabinet Office, Government of Japan (2006)

INDEX

A

absolute purchasing power parity, 58–59, 285

Abu Dhabi, 5, 43

acquisitions, 42, 220

adjustable peg systems, 3

    Bretton Woods System, 9–10

    definition, 283

adjustment mechanism, 7

    fixed exchange rate, 14

    with floating exchange rates, 13–16

    national current accounts, 5

Africa, 232

agriculture, 130–132

algorithmic trading, 134–135

American style options, 138, 139

    definition, 281

appreciation

    definition, 281

    and demand for currency, 49

arbitrage, 68, 281

Articles of Association, 243

ascending triangle pattern, 265

Asia, 232

Asian style options, 138

ask price. *see* offer price

asset price risk, 226

at the money (ATM), 139, 281

Australian dollar, 39, 198

    foreign exchange market share, 39, 41

Austria, 8

automated trading, 134–135

averaging, 201

B

back office operations, 83

baht, the, 27

balance of payments, 54–55

balance sheet hedging, 221

bank dealing limits. *see* dealing limits

Bank for International Settlements (BIS), 25

    Triennial central bank survey (2010), 38

bank notes, 37

Bank of England, 52–53

Bank of Thailand, 27

Banks

    commercial, 43–44

    as counterparties, 243

    foreign exchange market share, 44–45

    trading positions, 126

Barclays Bank, 44

Barclays Group BTOP FX Index, 198

barrier options, 166

base currency

    balance sheet hedging, 221

    definition, 281

    direct and indirect quotations, 69

    price quotations, 66–67

bear, 281

bear flag pattern, 267–268

bear spread, 281

bear squeeze, 281

bearish wedge pattern, 270

behavioural science, 252. *see also* psychology

benchmarking, 211

Bergsten, C. F., 5

bid, 281

bid currency, 284

    definition, 281

bid price, 65–66

    quoted in base currency, 66–67

    the spread, 67–68

bid rate, 281

bid-offer spread, 67–68, 209, 286

    and liquidity, 68

bills of exchange, 37

binary options, 166–167

black-box trading, 134–135

Y

Z